Creative Praise
SERIES

UNDER HIS WINGS

WARD PATTERSON

PSALMS 1-50

ACCENT BOOKS
Denver, Colorado

ACCENT BOOKS

A division of Accent Publications, Inc.
12100 West Sixth Avenue
P.O. Box 15337
Denver, Colorado 80215

Library of Congress Catalog Card Number 86-70646

ISBN 0-89636-216-7

INTRODUCTION

The Psalms are God's manual for praise and prayer. They are unique in Biblical literature in that they are inspired words from God that speak either about Him or are directed toward Him. In them God reveals to us divinely sanctioned patterns for adoration and praise.

This book grew out of a deep, personal need. I was aware that adoration and praise were to be a part of my prayer life. But I found that I did not really possess a vocabulary of praise. I tried to praise God in my prayers, but within a few minutes I invariably ran out of things to say about God to God. I had little trouble with intercession and petition. I could ask for things for others and for myself. Worship and thanksgiving, however, were another matter.

It dawned on me, at length, that I needed some schooling in the art of creative worship and praise. I needed some help with my prayer life. I needed to learn how to see the world as the psalmists saw it. I needed to learn how to speak to God about Himself.

With this in mind, I set about turning the Psalms into prayers. Many, of course, are already written as prayers. They are written in the second person and address God. Many others, however, are written in the third person and speak to others about God. I did not intend to paraphrase the Psalms so much as to elaborate on them. I wanted to personalize them, to make them relevant to the world I live in, to put them into words of my understanding. I did not seek to write them with an abundance of metaphor and simile. Rather, I wanted to take the metaphors already in the Psalms and elaborate upon their meanings. Using the Psalms as my inspiration, I wanted to let my mind rove in whatever direction it chose as I meditated on the words and allowed the thoughts of the psalm to send my thoughts flying wherever they would go.

I used a number of different versions as the basis for these prayer psalms. I made no attempt to record every concept in the psalm under consideration. Nor did I always use the order of the original. The long psalms were sometimes condensed, the short ones expanded. The purpose of the exercise was devotional. I did not struggle for exegetical meaning so much as I sought devotional enlightenment.

My purpose, in the beginning, was purely private. I wanted merely to experiment with a writing discipline that would improve my prayer life. I found that I enjoyed the project tremendously. Many times I could not stop with one or two psalms a day. The more I turned my mind to the nature of God, the more I wanted to praise Him. And the more I worked with His word, the more I delighted in it. The project became as addictive to me as jogging to a health nut. If I missed a day, I was disappointed. I looked forward each morning to the opportunity to sit down with my basement computer and speak God's words back to Him.

I began sharing my work with others. The wide range of emotions expressed in the Psalms guaranteed that the prayers would speak to a wide variety of human need. I began enclosing them in letters to friends. I began to read some as a part of our student worship services. Something, however, began to change as I began to use the prayers rhetorically. I had begun the project for private reasons, but more and more I began to use the psalms publicly. Almost without noticing it, I began to think of what others might think of my work more than to think of what God would think of it. I began, I must confess, to pray to be heard of men. It was turning into a writing project rather than a personal devotional exercise. And in so doing, it began losing some of its life and joy. While still feeling that the prayers might minister to others, I tried to remind myself that they were being addressed primarily to God and that my fundamental motive was to please Him.

The psalm/prayers in this book are published in hope that they will be used for private prayer and for public reading. I also hope that they will be used for comfort and encouragement. But most of all, I hope that they will cause others to undertake this same prayer project for themselves.

It is evident that the Psalms cover a wide range of emotion. The psalmist is often discouraged and bewildered, but the light of faith invariably breaks through the darkness of doubt and disappointment. God is not offended by our honest expressions of discouragement and bewilderment. It is hoped that the prayers of this book will minister to you in the unpredictable, changing circumstances of your life, and that they will enable you to speak to God honestly and openly about the tensions as well as the joys of your life.

PSALM 1

Father, fill me with Your blessings,
  for You alone can satisfy the longings of my heart.
Help me to walk in Your counsel,
  to know Your ways
    and follow them,
      not haphazardly or spasmodically,
       but patiently, consistently, fully.

Help me to block out the voices that urge me to disobedience.
  Help me to recognize that sin is an abomination to You.
Help me to rein in my desires for the forbidden,
  my longings for the deceits of this world.
Help me to live a separated life
  without being cut off
    from those You have called me to love in Your name.
Help me to know what to shun,
  what to do,
    what to say,
      where to go.
Help me to direct my thoughts to You.
  I am prone to dwell on the destructive
    and harbor hurt
      rather than fix my mind on You.
Help me to delight in Your Word to me.
  Help me to pause in the hurry of my life
    to reflect on Your promises,
      Your provision,
       and Your presence.

I know that when I meditate on Your Word,
  You refresh me.
    You relieve my pressures.
      You make my life fruitful.
        You keep me from spiritual drought.
       You give me ease in my tasks
        and the joy of accomplishment.

But I forget this too soon
　and I fall back into spiritual slothfulness.
　　My life becomes dry and lifeless.
　　　I am beset by doubts,
　　　　defeats,
　　　　　and emptiness.
　　　I feel condemned,
　　　　guilty,
　　　　　useless,
　　　　　　and crushed down.
　　　I just don't feel comfortable
　　　　with Your people anymore.

You know everything, O God.
　You know the way of truth and righteousness.
　　Let me walk with You!

I don't want to walk the way of futility and death.
　I want to walk with You by my side,
　　trusting You,
　　　and knowing You
　　　　as my Lord and Master.

AMEN

PSALM 2

Dear Lord, I know that those who oppose You are doomed to fail.
  They have their conferences,
    make their treaties,
      promote their plans,
        sign their alliances,
          and buy their arms,
            but their schemes will come to nothing.

There are always those who think
  that they are wiser and stronger than You.
They exalt themselves
  and defy You to act against them.
    They take Your name in vain,
      and persecute Your people,
        and ridicule Your laws,
          and oppose Your purposes.
They think that they are the center of the world
  and that You are impotent to bring them to task.
    They laugh at those who trust in You
      and take pride in their knowledge and accomplishments.

It must look ridiculous to You—
  man's pretentious boasting.
    How do You keep from laughing out loud?
      We are such haughty creatures,
        always taking credit for the things we do
          and forgetting that You are the creator of all.
      We think that we have everything under control,
        that we've mastered the secrets of this universe,
          that we no longer need You,
            and that we are capable of sitting on Your throne.
  Yet, I know that just a word from You
    changes everything.
        You can turn all our little enterprises into chaos.
          A word from You
            and both we and our projects are gone.

You are involved in this world.
  You have uplifted and upheld
    those who have honored Your name.
      You have treated us
        with all the love of a father for his children.
You have chosen to enter into human history
  in Your Son, Jesus.
    You have held nothing back
      from those who walk faithfully with You.
        We are possessors of all the goodness of life.
You are not a passive observer in the affairs of humankind.
  You will destroy the wicked
    and exalt the faithful.

Help our leaders to know the source of true security,
  strength, and wisdom.
Help our legislators to be more concerned with principle
  than with popularity.
Help our judges to be more concerned with justice
  than with rights.
Help us all to know that You alone
  are worthy of our trust.
Help us to serve You wholeheartedly,
  deeply,
    respectfully,
      joyfully,
        exuberantly,
         consistently,
          loyally,
           reverently.
Help me to be worthy of Your favor
  and to commit to You all that I am and have.
    You are a great God!
      Thank You for loving and preserving me.

AMEN

PSALM 3

Lord, I'm surrounded by trouble.
　Everywhere I look I see those who are set against me.
　　Their eyes are filled with scorn
　　　and their lips speak slander.
　They say You are dead
　　and that I'm a fool to rely on You.
　They say that this life is all there is
　　and that my hope in You is fantasy.

But I know differently.
　I've experienced Your protection.
　　I've been lifted up when I've been down.
　　　I've been blessed and strengthened by Your love.
　You have answered my prayers.
　　When I've cried out in despair,
　　　You have heard and responded.
　You have given me peace in the midst of danger.
　　You have given me rest, sustenance,
　　　joy, and hope.
　You have banished fear from my life.
　　I face each day with optimism
　　　because I know Your salvation,
　　　　Your protection,
　　　　　and Your vindication.

Lord, help me to ignore the taunts of my enemies.
　Help me to keep my eyes on You and Your blessings.
　　Help me to live and pray in confidence of Your help.
　　　Help me to rest in Your protection.
　　　　Help me to undertake noble things in Your name.
　　　　Help me to be bold and fearless.
　　　　　Help me to rely on Your might to fight for right.

Lord, You are my deliverance and salvation.
　You fill my life with blessing.
　　Thank You, Lord.

AMEN

PSALM 4

O Lord, I'm calling on Your name again.
    You are the source of all that is good in my life.
        You are my benefactor, comforter, and deliverer.
    You have raised me up before.
        When I was in the pits,
            You lifted up my spirits
                and delivered me from anguish.
    You protected me from misfortune
        and kept me from falling victim to my enemies.
    You heard my prayers and responded with love.

So, here I am again,
    throwing myself on Your mercy,
        asking You to listen,
            seeking Your help,
                trusting You to respond to my need.

I know that I don't deserve Your favor.
    I don't add much luster to the glory of Your name.
        So often I chase after things that are empty and useless.
        I'm often distracted, disinterested, and disarrayed.
    I'm taken in by lies and contribute my own deceptions
        to the falsehood that saturates my world.

I know that in my humanity I'm unworthy of Your concern.
    I have such a tendency toward sinful waywardness.
        I'm rebellious and deceitful,
            undependable and ambitious
                for all the wrong things.

But You treat the godly with gracious love.
    You answer the prayers of the upright
        and respond to the entreaties of the faithful.
I cannot help but stand in awe of Your lovingkindness.
    Just thinking of You makes sin unattractive.
Night and day I think of You and know Your peace.

Sometimes my mind turns to You as I lie upon my bed.
  I experience a stillness and tranquillity
    that restores Your harmony to my anxious thoughts.
  I know the warmth of communion with You
    and sense a quiet release from the tensions that trouble me.

I would bring to You a heart that desires Your favor!
  I would trust You with my longings.
    I would commit to You my fears.
I would seek to lay before You a righteous life
  and a contrite heart
    and a submissive spirit.

The world is peopled with skeptics and unbelievers
  who accuse You of ignoring the hurts and injustices of the world.
    They don't expect You
      to become involved with the affairs of mankind.
    They are both inside the church and outside the church.
    They expect things just to happen as they will,
      and they don't expect
        prayer to make
          any difference whatsoever.
    They wring their hands,
      and weep their tears,
        and prophesy impending doom,
          but never look to You for comfort and hope.

Yet I know that You look on us with favor
  and that You seek to illuminate the darkness
    of our fears with the light of Your tender mercy.

You look on us with sympathy and feel the ache of our anxieties.
  You desire to fill our lives with satisfaction and joy.
    You want us to experience *every day* the joy of payday,
      the newness of honeymoon,
        the satisfaction of vacation,
          the contentment of bountiful harvest,
            the gladness of newfound friendship.

Though often surrounded by fears, doubts, defeats, and dangers,
    I can lie down in peace and sleep in childlike innocence.
I have no need for tranquilizers for You are my peace.
    I can rest beneath Your arms of safety
        and rise to meet each new day with hope.

O Lord, I thank You that You are a God
    who hears my prayers and responds to my needs.
        I thank You for Your incomparable character,
            Your loving deliverance,
                Your tender mercy,
                    and Your continuous attention to my prayers.
        I ask that You will open my eyes
            to see Your careful attention on my behalf.
        Help me to seek after You with all my heart.
            Help me to turn my back on vanity and imitation
            and to meditate quietly.
I know You have a special relationship
    with those who respond to Your love.
        You hearken to their prayers,
            and grant relief with a capital "R"
                to those who orient their lives toward You.
        You listen to their night meditations
            and grant the sleep of peace
                and the rest of reassurance.
I want that for my life!

Therefore, I offer my life on Your altar
    and trust You with all that I am and wish to be.
I will close my ears to those who ridicule my faith
    and declare that my hope in You is wishful thinking.
With diligence, I will seek Your favor.
    With gladness, I will know Your beneficence.
        With peace, I will know Your deliverance.
O Lord, thank You for watching me through my nights.
    And thank You for making my day!

AMEN

PSALM 5

Lord, I ask You to listen to my words of prayer
  and my thoughts of adoration.
    I'm slowly, so slowly, learning to pray,
      and I have so much still to learn.
    Please listen to what I have to say.
      Please respond to the deep yearnings of my heart.

You are my King and I seek Your uncontested rule
  in the whole of my life.
    You are my God,
      and I would make You supreme in all my desires.
I trust Your counsel, for there is no one else to whom I can turn
  for comfort, assurance, direction, and meaning.
I would begin each day of my life
  with a prayer of praise and thanksgiving.
I would greet each dawn with contemplation of Your majesty.
  I would lift up my eyes and my heart to Your throne of mercy
    and utter words of admiration and entreaty.

When I wake to each new day, I want my first thoughts to be of You.
  I want my spirit to be tuned to Your frequency
    and my heart to be programmed to Your operating system.
I would seek Your approval in my projects.
  before I lock them into my desires.
    I would pursue Your counsel
      before I commit myself to my plans and goals.
I would acknowledge Your superiority and sovereignty
  in all my thoughts and actions.

I know from Your Word that You abhor wickedness.
  You have no place in Your nature for sin and rebellion.
    You are a God who takes pleasure in goodness
      and who resists evil and perversion.
I know that I must choose the way of virtue.
  I cannot expect You to bless me when I stray from Your path.
    You cannot tolerate iniquity and immorality.

You turn Your wrath against those who use their lips for lying,
   their hands to shed blood,
      their minds to deceive the unwary,
      and their bodies to abuse others.

Knowing all this, I want to be a person of righteousness.
   I want to be a person of sincere faith,
      and loving worship,
      and resolute goodness.
   In the face of my own waywardness,
      I want to know Your mercy.
   I want to have the right heart attitude toward You—
      fear, awe, respect,
         honor, reverence,
            praise, and thanksgiving.
Help me to accomplish this, O Lord.
   Lead me in Your ways.
      Keep me from the abominations of those who are around me.
         Help me to stay on the straight and narrow path.
      Keep me from digressions,
         detours,
            and delays.

Don't let me be taken in by my sinful society.
   There are so many who speak against You,
      whose lives are given over to all that You condemn,
         whose minds are filled continually with evil.
   They write their bestsellers,
      congratulate themselves on their enlightenment,
         and boast of their liberation from Your commandments.

Don't let them get away with it, O Lord!
   Make their folly known to all.
      Ensnare them with their own traps.
         Turn their counsel against them,
            and devour them by their own foolishness.

Treat them as they deserve, and make their downfall evident to all.
  Bring down their financial empires,
    expose their foolishness,
      bring home to them the consequences of their folly.

But let those who trust in You experience Your joy!
  Save them from the tragedies that might otherwise befall them.
    With Your truth, defend them from deception.
      With Your shield, keep them from harm.
        With Your favor, bless them.
          With Your love, encompass them.

Help me to be the kind of person who trusts in You,
  who shouts aloud with joy to You,
    who experiences and notes ministrations by You,
      and who draws hope and confidence from You.

For You are a God who listens to my prayers,
  who despises my sin,
    who holds me accountable for my wrongs,
      who shows mercy to my contrition,
        and who receives my worship with grace.
  You lead me when I seek Your counsel,
    You give me knowledge when I bend my heart to worship You.
Though you leave the wicked to the destruction of their own folly,
  You bring me gladness because I have put my trust in You.
You are with me when I pursue righteousness,
  to bless and to protect.

Help me to be Your kind of person—
  and reflect Your matchless love!

AMEN

PSALM 6

Lord, please pardon my waywardness
  and forgive my sins.
    Don't treat me as I deserve.
      Don't bring on me the trials that discipline
       and the difficulties that punish.

Have mercy on me, O Lord,
  for right now I've about had it.
    I ache all over.
      My spirit sags.
      I'm devastated.
        I just can't cope any longer.
          I can't laugh or sing anymore.
          My problems overpower me.
            My mind and my body cry out for relief.
           My thoughts are filled with pain.
          I can't eat or sleep.
            Everything is falling apart.
             I don't think I can go on!
  There just seems to be no end to it all.
    I weep in anguish.
      My problems won't go away.
        My face is drawn and my eyes are glazed.
        I'm worn out,
          beaten down,
            overpowered,
           depressed,
             discouraged,
             defeated,
              dejected,
              downcast,
               dispirited,
                melancholy,
                blue.
  I call out in my pain and anguish.
  I'm weary of heart and feel like I want to die.

Keep these self-destructive thoughts from me, O Lord.
We both know my death will bring You no praise.
The grave is no place for shouts of thanksgiving!
I can't sleep!
My pillow is soaked with tears.
My covers are thrown off by my thrashing.
My eyes are dim and red from weeping.
They are drawn back into their sockets,
puffy, dark, and hollowed.
I can't seem to escape from my difficulties.
They stalk me like living foes,
unremittingly dogging my footsteps.
They are like enemy agents
spying out my weakness in order to destroy me utterly.
They cling to me tenaciously,
and consume my every thought.
They sap my strength, disconcerting and devouring me.

Please, Lord, bring an end to it.
Turn me around.
Lift me up.
Hear my prayers and restore me to gladness.
Return me to spiritual and physical health.
Heal my brokenness and bewilderment.
Shower me with Your unfailing love.
Refresh me with Your renewal.
Arm me with Your power.
Overcome the enemies of my peace.
Help me to praise You once again.

But, Lord, I think I am beginning
to sense Your presence in all of this.
I know that You have heard my weeping
and that You are prepared to deliver me.
I know that You are responding to my plea for mercy
and that You have heard my anguished prayer.

The tide seems to be turning.
The dawn seems to be breaking.

The rainbow is appearing from the thunderclouds.
My heart is experiencing peace.
The ache is abating.
The joy is returning.

O Lord, thank You for sharing in my blues.
Thank You for not casting me off
when I live with defeat rather than victory.
Thank You for showing me mercy
rather than wrath,
for showing me love
rather than anger
in my times of doubt and defeat.

Thank You for hearing my groans,
responding to my cries,
wiping away my tears,
accepting my imperfect prayers.
Thank You for putting to flight the foes,
that war with me inside and out.
Thank You for bringing them to naught,
for weakening their stranglehold on my life,
for delivering me from their painful grasp.
Thank You for standing by me and hearing.
Oh, thank You, Lord, for hearing!

AMEN

PSALM 7

O Lord, my God, I hide myself in You.
  I can trust You to save me
    from all that endangers.
  Deliver me from my adversaries.
    They stalk me like wild beasts,
      determined to tear me to pieces.
    They would drag me into their den
      and devour me for their pleasure.
    They have set their hearts on my destruction
      and cannot wait to do me ill.
  And there seems to be no one to defend me.
    Nobody takes my side.
      No one faces the foe with me.
        Nobody fights for my cause.
          No one snatches me from the jaws of the lion.

Lord, if I am at fault,
  I accept what befalls as Your righteous judgment.
    If I have done wrong to my neighbor,
      if I have done evil to my friend,
        or if I have been unjust to my enemy,
          then let my foes prevail.
    If I am guilty of wrongdoing,
      it is just that You should punish me.
        If I am guilty before You,
          it is proper that You take the side of my enemies
            and trample my name in the dust.
              It is even right that You take my life,
                if You so choose.

But that does not seem to be the case just now.
  So I call upon You to come to my aid,
    to mobilize Your might against my foes,
      and to vindicate my name with Your just support.
  Exercise Your rule over all people.
    Judge me according to Your standard of righteousness.

I sincerely believe that I am not at fault in this matter.
   Though I am far from perfect,
      my integrity can stand Your scrutiny.
   I've searched my heart and my actions
      for any indication that my foes may be Your
         instruments of justice,
            but I have found nothing
               to merit Your condemnation.

O righteous God,
   You know my mind and heart.
      Please bring an end to the things that frighten me.
      Turn away the violence of the wicked.
         Make my life once again secure and peaceful.
I throw myself on Your mercy.
   I trust You to intervene
      to save the pure and upright.
   I expect You to exercise Your wrath against the wicked.

I know that Your patience can be pushed only so far.
   There will come a time when You will no longer wait.
      Your sword is sharp and ready,
         Your bow is stretched taut,
            Your deadly, flaming arrows are ready
               and poised for release upon the workers of iniquity.

I know the way of evil, O God Most High.
   It turns on the one who practices it.
      Wrongdoers conceive their vicious plans,
         become pregnant with malevolence,
            and give birth to treachery and falsehood.
They devise their traps
   and are ensnared by them.
      Everything boomerangs on them.
         Violence committed against others returns to haunt them.
The pits they dig to waylay others cave in on their own heads.

I can trust You to bring these things to pass.
   I know that You are by my side in my difficulties.
      I know that evil cannot overcome me,
         and that I will come through this hard time
            strengthened and victorious.
I thank You for Your righteous nature
   that will not allow the noble to fall.
      I want You to know how much I love and trust You,
         my deliverer, my shelter,
            my defender, my justifier,
               my judge, my security,
                  my savior, my avenger, my guardian.
   I will sing Your praises in the midst of my trials.
   I will lift my voice in tribute to Your name.

I am learning that such times as this
   teach me to rely on You
      and to rejoice regardless of my circumstances.

You have replaced my fear with the song of triumph.
   You have given me confidence
      that all will turn out well in the end.

Thank You, O Lord.
   Thank You!
      Thank You!
         Thank You!
            Thank You!
               Thank You!
                  Thank You!
                     Thank You!
                        Thank You!
                           Thank You!
                              Thank You!
                                 Thank You!
                                    Thank You!
                                       Thank You!
                                          Thank You!

AMEN

PSALM 8

O Lord, my Lord, how wonderful You are!
Your majesty is in everything I behold.
Your glory is proclaimed in the whole of creation.
The heavens and the earth
combine to proclaim Your greatness.

You establish Your grandeur from weakness and dependency.
From the lips of infants and children
expressions of praise spring forth.
How often I have heard the profoundest wisdom
from the lips of small children!

Your glory puts to shame those who oppose You
and silences those who mock.
I see it in the heavens
where the vast expanse of space proclaims Your enormity.
Billions of stars proclaim Your workmanship,
moving in their galaxies,
sending forth their light,
and illuminating my night sky.
You have set the moon in its orbit,
reflecting into my night a message of Your glory,
sending onto my shores the surging tides,
and directing my thoughts to love.
Everything moves according to Your plan.
Everything hangs in space by Your word.
Everything holds together by Your might.

When I look up, I feel so small.
I'm just a little human on the face of a tiny planet.
And yet, sometimes I think that everything
in the whole universe revolves around me.
I fix my eyes on my ambitions,
my troubles, my accomplishments, and my failures,
and I act as if the universe
is holding its breath in expectation.

But the heavens put me in my place.
They remind me of how insignificant I really am.
They reduce me to realistic proportions
and remind me that I am unworthy of Your lovingkindness.
It amazes me that You who made the whole universe,
with its infinite miles of space
and its gigantic celestial bodies,
are interested in my affairs.

But, amazingly, You are!
You have given me a high position in Your concerns.
You have made me just a little lower than the angels.
You have given me worth and dignity
and afforded me a place of significance
in Your divine scheme of things.
You have given me a mind to reason,
plan, discover, analyze, and predict.
You have made me in Your image,
a creating, responding, living, and loving being.
You have given me dominance
over all creatures on the face of the earth.
You have given me a hand with dexterity,
and a mind to overcome my physical limitations.
You have given me the capacity
to transform the raw materials of this world
into instruments for my use.
I sometimes take undue credit for my technologies,
not acknowledging that all my inventiveness depends on You
and on the raw materials You have placed in this world.
Thank You, Lord, for the wonders of the heavens and the earth.
Thank You for the reminders they are of Your greatness.

O Lord, my Lord, how wonderful You are!
Your majesty is in everything I behold.
Your glory is proclaimed in the whole of creation.
The heavens and the earth
combine to proclaim Your greatness!

AMEN

PSALM 9

O Lord, I want to praise You with all that I am.
I want to speak of Your wonderful deeds in my life.
I want to rejoice in Your greatness
and sing Your praise with thanksgiving.

You have protected me from the evil that lies in wait for me.
You have kept me from harm.
You have defended me with Your strength.
You have executed judgment on the wicked
and extended mercy to the righteous.
The nations that fear You have been blessed,
and the nations that have opposed You have fallen.
The greatness of the wicked has vanished away
and their citadels are broken and empty.
Their leaders have perished
and their fame is remembered no more.
But You are remembered, O Lord.
Your throne of judgment does not pass away.
You judge the world in righteousness
and govern the affairs of men with equity.
You show compassion on the oppressed
and reach out in love to the broken.
You are dependable, gracious, and trustworthy altogether.
You do not turn Your back on those who reach out to You.

I will sing Your praises on the mountaintops.
I will mention Your name with reverence
and tell of Your mighty acts in history.
You note what happens in human affairs.
You will avenge those who are mistreated,
tortured and starved,
humiliated and dispossessed,
intimidated and mutilated by the wicked.
You know who my oppressors are, O Lord.
You know what is in their heads and hearts
and how far they go to do me ill.

Please help me.
  Lift up my sagging spirits.
    Draw me back from the depths of depression.
      Save me from the slow death of ridicule.
  Have mercy on me.

I will give You the credit for all the good that comes.
  I will constantly recount Your attention to my needs.
  I will shout Your glory from the housetops,
    and broadcast Your praise to all who pass by.

Those who are Yours are recognized for their justice.
  They partake of Your nature and are upright.
But the wicked constantly devise diabolical schemes.
  They seek to do harm to others,
    but are the victims of their own plots.
  Your justice always prevails in the end.

Those who forget You, my Lord,
  will be brought down.
    They will perish in their rebellions.
You are not impressed by the arrogance of worldly might,
  but You do reach out to the needy and afflicted.

The time has come, O Lord,
  for You to come with judgment.
    Bring to naught the pretensions of evildoers.
      Bring judgment upon those who work iniquity.
Show them that they are finite human beings.
  Expose their frailty.
    Bring them to their knees.
      Humble them before You.

O Lord, I pray that my nation
  might not be the object of Your wrath.
    I pray that this country might remember You.
      Forgive us for drifting so far away
        from dependence on You.

We build our bombs,
    and bottle our nerve gas,
        and test our missiles.
We arrogantly assume that our nation is the center of the earth.
    We squander our resources,
        boast of our greatness,
            and flaunt our affluence.
We oppress the poor,
    discriminate against minorities,
        and corrupt the young.
Yet wickedness goes unchecked
    in every aspect of our communal life.
        Our homes are breaking up,
            our cities are unsafe at night,
                our government is corrupt,
                    and our schools do not acknowledge You.

O God, turn us again to the way of truth and righteousness.
    Give us indignation
        over evil that is deceptively packaged as enlightenment.
Help us, as our coins say, to put our trust in You.
    Help us to lean on You in our weakness
        and draw our principles
            for life and government from Your Word.
Have mercy upon us, O Lord.
    Be gracious to us, Most Holy Father.
        Help us to be a nation that honors You,
            so that You need not turn Your judgment upon us.
Protect us from evil.
    Deliver us from deceit.
    Keep us secure in Your strength.

O Lord, may our nation praise You with all aspects of its life.
    Help it to honor Your wonderful name by its every action.
        Help it to rejoice in Your greatness
            and to sing Your praises
                with unending gratitude and thanksgiving.

AMEN

PSALM 10

Lord, sometimes it seems like You stand aloof
  from all the troubles in this world.
    It seems as if evil is allowed to prosper
      while You stand silent and unconcerned.
  The world is filled with bullies
    who delight in pushing others around.
    It is peopled with terrorists,
      and rapists,
        and child molesters,
          and wife beaters,
            and thieves,
              and juvenile delinquents,
                and those who prey on the old and helpless.

Some of these users and abusers of people
  seem so respectable.
    They live in their mansions,
      jet to Europe,
        and seem able to buy whatever they please.
  They gain fame and squander fortunes
    on their insatiable cravings.
    They brag of their conquests,
      and boast of their excesses,
        and take pride in their fleshly indulgence.
  They glorify vice
    and enjoy the fruits of their vicious exploitation of others.

They propagate their corruption
  and distribute their filth as if it were art.
    They glorify wickedness
      and ridicule virtue.
      They delight in abusing Your name,
        and doing ill to those who love You.
        They are very proud of their accomplishments.
  They feel no need of Your help
    and consider themselves self-made wonders.

They have no room in their lives
  for You and Your teaching.
    Rather, they consider themselves the standard
      for good and bad.
        They see their prosperity and advantage
          as the only "right."
            They are a law unto themselves,
              and defy anyone to tell them what to do.
They think they are above Your laws
  and that they have no need of anything You have to offer.
They believe that things will always work out to their profit
  and that they will always come out on top.
They have no conscience about their wrongdoing
  and the harm it inflicts on others.

Their mouths are foul.
  They use words to wound,
    intimidate, defraud,
      deceive, ridicule,
        divide, manipulate,
          ensnare, and kill.
Trouble follows them everywhere.
  They are a fountain of evil,
    filth, and malignancy.
They are always hatching new plots
  to ambush the unwary.
    They peddle their drugs,
      and prey on the addicts.
        They serve their drinks,
          and prowl the night
            looking for pickups,
              or easy marks,
                or runaway children,
                  or defenseless victims.
They give their minds totally over
  to plotting and scheming new ways to
    defraud, bilk, and embezzle.

They are not always to be found
  in the sleazy parts of society.
    They sometimes live in huge mansions
      and move in respectable business circles.
    They don't seem to care whom they hurt.
      It is all a game to them.
        The point is to be smart,
          and quick,
            and unprincipled.
    What does it matter that others are crushed
      by their greed?

Such people are convinced
  that You are blind to their evil.
    They are sure You don't exist
      because they get away with so much.
    They do not know that You are watching.
They think You are impotent
  in the face of their wickedness.

Lord, don't let them get away with this.
  Don't abandon the helpless.
    Don't let the wicked revile Your name without consequence.
Call them to an accounting.
  Show them that You are not to be ignored or flaunted.
Don't leave the weak to fend for themselves.
  In particular, be with those who have no
    one to protect them,
      the fatherless and the widows.

Break the stranglehold of vice
  that fuels the ruthless and heartless.
Strike them with Your hand.
  Call them to reckoning!
    Expose to the humiliation of public scrutiny
      those who thought their corruption
        was well covered.

Make an example of them.
   Entrap them in the mire of their
      own evil plots.
Bring down those governments
   that terrorize their citizens,
      that rule by violence and terror,
         and that exploit the poor and defenseless.
Do not let those who brainwash,
   brutalize,
      and badger
         escape unpunished.

You are sovereign God!
   All things are in Your hand.
      You will be here after human despots
         and "godfathers"
            and "kingpins"
               have been destroyed.
Nations and people will rise and fall,
   but You are everlasting.

You are merciful and loving toward the outcast,
   the weak,
      the abused,
         the dispossessed,
            the exploited,
               and the afflicted.
You lift them up, and draw them to Your breast.
   You wipe away their tears,
      and heal their wounds,
         and bind up their sorrows.
            Their cries come to Your ears.
You move to shelter the innocent,
   the lonely,
      and the unprotected.
You know the brutality of man to man
   and his propensity for terror.

I trust You to champion the defenseless
and to bring the oppressors to justice.

Father, it is easy for me to get morally indignant
at the things I see other people doing.
To look at the daily papers
and to listen to the evening news
is to be reminded again and again
of man's bent toward evil.
And I can always point out *others* who
are extremely wicked and deserve Your wrath.
But You know that I too am guilty before You.
I too take advantage of others when it suits my purposes.
I too am tempted to misrepresent for my advantage.
I too am guilty of greed,
exploitation and shortchanging,
covetousness and pride,
arrogance and scheming,
lust and blasphemy,
idolatry and self-glorification,
falsehood and opportunism,
evil speaking and oppression.
Forgive me, Father!
Help me to be as concerned with the sins of my life
as I am with the sins of others.
Help me to cast out the sawlog in my own eye
so that I can see to help clear
the sawdust from my brother's eye.
Bring each of us
to repentance and renewal.

Turn this world from evil, my Father.
Start with me!

AMEN

PSALM 11

O Lord, I put my trust in You.
  You are my high place,
    my refuge,
      my fortress,
        and my deliverance.

Sometimes I feel caught in the crossfire of the wicked.
  They have me in their sights
    and have their fingers on their triggers.
      They seek to destroy me.

But You are my bunker.
  You encompass me with Your strong bulwarks.
    You hold me in the palm of Your hand.
      You help me keep my footing
        in the fight.
You oversee my battles.
  From Your throne in the heavens,
    You look down on my struggles,
      and analyze my actions.

You strengthen me through my tests,
  so long as I am stedfast
    in doing what is right.
      But You are against me when I set my ways
        in the paths of wickedness and violence.

Wickedness is set for destruction.
  You send the wicked deceit,
    burning lust,
      fiery ordeals,
        consuming desires.
Their lives are tossed about,
  unsettled,
    insecure,
      and unsteady.

But the righteous receive Your blessing,
   You look with favor on their lives
      and shower them with Your benefits.

Help me to walk with the righteous,
   to put my trust in You,
      and to rest in You.

Lift me above the fray,
   deliver me from deeds of unrighteousness,
      protect me from the consequences of wickedness.
   I long, more than anything else in the world,
      to receive Your love and approval.

AMEN

PSALM 12

I want to cry "Help!", O Lord.

Everywhere I look there is wickedness.
  It comes to me on my TV screen,
    enticing me with unbridled sexuality,
      luring me with messages of indulgence,
        laughing at my values,
          ridiculing righteousness.
It seems as if good people come off as hypocrites,
  windbags, or crazies.

The pornographers build their mansions,
  and the beer companies own their stadiums,
    and the drug dealers fill their Swiss bank accounts.
They are proud in their prosperity.
  They speak vanity as if it were wisdom.
    Their works are debased and the imagination
      of their minds is given to the promotion of evil.
They gather in their bars,
  boast of their conquests,
    and pride themselves in their freedom.
  They corrupt one another,
    prey on the weak and innocent,
      slander the pure.
  They lure into addiction,
    destroy for profit,
      abuse for pleasure.
"We are our own gods," they exult.
  "We are our own judges," they shout.
    "We are our own lords," they proclaim.
      "We are our own laws," they boast.
"Who cares that we degrade men and women,
  take the money of the poor,
    debase the nation, corrupt the young,
      fill the streets with rape, the schools with violence,
        and the jails with broken lives?"

YOU CARE, O LORD!
   You see!
      You know!

You have promised to watch over those who trust in You.
   I can live with optimism,
      and joy,
         and hope
            because of You.

The words of the evil are putrid,
   but Your words are pure.
The thoughts of the corrupt are depraved,
   but Your thoughts are righteous.

I will cast my lot with You, O God!
   You will preserve me.
      Long after the wicked have destroyed one another,
         and choked on their greed,
            and burned themselves out in their lust,
               squandered their wealth, and lost their loved ones,
   You and I will be together.

You have promised to sustain those who love You.
   Though the wicked surround me on every side,
      and evil seems to succeed,
   You are still Lord of the universe.
      In You alone is meaning and lasting success.
         I will rely on You.
You are my peace, my strength,
   my preservation, my truth,
      my liberation, my provider,
         my safety, my guide,
            my purifier, my exaltation.
You are my ever-present help, O Lord.
   In You I trust.

AMEN

PSALM 13

Sometimes, O Lord, I feel as if You have forgotten me.
I feel as if I am alone in my troubles
and You are nowhere to be found.

I come to You in prayer,
but my words seem to speak only to myself.
I seek Your consolation,
but my pain does not go away.
I try to understand,
but my bewilderment remains.

You seem far away,
unconcerned,
unsympathetic,
callous.
I begin to doubt that I ever really knew You.
I begin to suspect that my joy in You
was no more than wishful thinking.
I begin to fear that either You don't care,
or You really don't exist at all.

I cry out in my despair.
I seek resolution for my doubts.
I search for meaning.
I grope for truth.
I weep for understanding.

But my troubles do not go away.
My adversaries continue to prosper.
My oppressors remain in control.
My sickness persists.
My weakness renders me helpless.
My failures compound themselves.
My depression grows.
I just don't have the will to go on.
I feel as if I am going to die.

There seems no end to my suffering.
  I can't seem to get out of my rut of self-pity.
    Others shun me because of my pessimism.
Those who try to comfort me only make me feel worse.
  They mouth their platitudes.
    "It is all working together for good," they say.
      "Turn to the Lord and pray."
        "It will all work out."
  They say they understand,
    but they don't.

I am cold,
  tired,
    bewildered,
      beaten down,
        hopeless,
          mired,
            defeated,
              drained,
                broken.
Lord, hear me!
Hear me, O Lord!

Lighten my load.
  Lift me up from my despair.
    Bring understanding to my soul.
      Restore the joy of life
        and the anticipation of the future I once knew.
Don't let me be a bad advertisement
  for the Christian life.
Don't let me be such that people will point at me
  and criticize You, whom I have trusted.

Please, Lord,
  don't let evil triumph.
    Don't let the wicked go unpunished.
      Don't let those who beat me down succeed.
        Don't let them take joy in my sorrow.

Though I am in the depths,
   I cry out to You in the heights.
      I do trust in Your mercy.
         I do rejoice in Your salvation.
I know that my relationship with You
   does not depend on my success.
      I know that when I am emotionally down
         You do not turn away from me.

You have called me to eternal life.
   You will not abandon me now.
You bring joy in the midst of tears,
   renewal in the midst of despair,
      strength in the midst of defeat,
         hope in the midst of discouragement.

I *will* rejoice,
   even though I don't feel like it.
I *will* sing,
   though my heart breaks within me.
I *will* trust,
   though I cannot understand.
I *will* remember
   Your bountiful providence in my life,
      covering me with good,
         remembering me when I feel alone and helpless.

I *know* You have not forgotten.

   Don't let me forget that!

AMEN

PSALM 14

Lord, there is always an abundance of scoffers.
  They jeer that You do not exist
    and that my faith in You is based on myths.
  They do not subject themselves to Your Word,
    and they go their way ignoring Your sovereignty.
  They have no conscience about doing evil,
    and their corruption permeates our society.
How foolish they are!

I know that You look down on Your world
  and search the hearts of all people.
    You know those who seek You
      and who walk in Your ways.
And You know also those who walk the wayward paths.
  They are corruption personified,
    always doing evil and plotting iniquity.
  They are ignorant of You and Your will.
    Your name is on their lips only for cursing,
      never for prayer.
  They use their mouths, not for Your adoration,
    but to bite and devour one another.
      They live in pride
        when they ought to live in fear.

But You, O Lord, look after the poor and the innocent,
  the very ones evildoers seek to cheat and exploit.
You are their refuge and strength.
  Put the parasites to flight.
    Upset their schemes.
      Don't let them prevail.
Oh, that Your people might execute Your will,
  that Your goodness might be seen in all our actions,
    and that Your righteousness
      might flow from our lives of worship.
Turn our hearts again to joy in You.
  Help us to find Your peace and gladness.

Lord, sometimes I'm so foolish.
  I get weary with well doing.
    I begin to doubt Your watchcare and concern.
      I get my eyes on the things of this earth
        rather than on the things of Your kingdom.
I make myself God
  and follow my every whim and desire.
    I exalt myself in my conceit
      and rebel against Your authority.
I begin to relax my ethical standards
  and compromise my principles
    for the approval of men.
I think I can get along without Your direction,
  and I become tolerant of sin in my life.
    I live without consulting You
      and dabble in hypocrisy and duplicity.

I know how deceitful I can become,
  deceitful with You,
    deceitful with others,
      deceitful with myself.
I ignore my prayer life
  and begin to rely on my own ability
    to work things out.
I scheme for my advantage
  and abuse those who get in my way.

Forgive me, Father,
  and help me to get things back on track.
    I *know* You are displeased with me
      and that I cannot live with Your blessing
        so long as I am in rebellion
        and ignore Your will.

Help me to return to the joy of my salvation,
  to the gladness of Your presence in my life.

O Lord, give me wisdom!
  Give me assurance of Your love
    and pleasure in Your people.
      Give me confidence in You,
        knowledge of Your ways,
          joy in Your presence,
            hope in Your providence.

Lord, I cannot live without You!
  We both know that,
    but I am so prone to forget.
Give me Your wisdom,
  for You alone are the source of enlightenment
    to my darkened mind and heart.

AMEN

PSALM 15

Lord, I want to put my life on a firm foundation.
  I want to stand uprightly before You.
    I want to be resolute,
      strong, firm,
        dependable, secure.
  I know that You condemn the wicked
    and honor those who fear You.
  I know the things that displease You—
    a spiteful, brutal,
      gossiping, cutting,
        slanderous tongue,
      unloving actions toward my neighbors,
        greed at the expense of others.
Help me to shun these things.

I know, too, the things that please You—
  righteous conduct,
    purity of heart,
      obedience to Your will.

Help me to live uprightly,
  work righteously,
    and think truthfully.
Help me to keep my tongue from evil
  and to be thoughtful of my neighbors.
Help me to fear You
  and to keep Your Word,
    and to use my material resources to honor You.

Help me not to take advantage of others,
  nor to satisfy my greed at the expense of others.
Help me to live my life in nearness to You,
  to be a person of integrity and holy honor,
    and to be a person of my word.
Help me to be the kind of person
  I, as well as others, can respect.

Help me to put away grudges,
  jealousy,
    and selfishness.
Help me to tell the truth
  when it is not to my advantage to do so.
Help me to be more interested
  in generosity than in gain.

Help me to be more interested
  in aiding others
    than in advancing my fortunes.
Help me to be strong,
  resolute,
    uncorrupted,
      uncompromising,
        and immovable
          in my resolve
            to live righteously.
Help me to be committed to truth,
  kindness,
    generosity,
      loyalty,
        and liberality.

AMEN

PSALM 16

O God, You are my safety,
  my refuge, my security,
    my benefactor, my counselor,
      my guide, my strength, and my hope.
        You are my Lord,
          the source of all good.
You delight in those who are truly Yours,
  in those who are set aside to Your ways.

I know the futility of following other gods.
  I am committed to You alone.
    I will keep myself from idolatry
      and enjoy Your sovereignty in the whole of my life.
You fill my life with good
  and confer on me Your legacy of delight.
    You counsel me
      in the daytime and in the night.
You lead me
  in the strength of Your might.

Because of You my life is filled with gladness,
  and my lips speak forth words of joy.
    I am at peace,
      secure in Your watchcare over me.
You will never abandon me to death,
  nor forsake me into destruction.
Rather, You make known to me the path of life,
  so that You can fill me with joy
    and the pleasures of Your good favor.

You are my Lord,
  the source of all good.
You delight in those who are truly Yours,
  in those who are set aside to Your ways.

Delight in me!

AMEN

PSALM 17

O Lord, I want to pray in righteousness,
  and speak to You from a heart that is true.
Please listen to my call,
  respond to my yearnings,
    and put to rest my fears.

I want to call on You from a heart
  that can stand Your scrutiny.
    I want my prayers to rise from a life
      that has no hidden pockets of hypocrisy.
    Whether You examine me at night or in the day,
      I am resolved that You will find
        no evil in my mind or mouth.
  In the midst of the tests of my life,
    I want to be an example of faithfulness and trust.
  I simply want to speak my prayers from a mouth of integrity.

I've tried to keep myself from wickedness.
  I haven't run with the wrong crowd.
  I haven't taken advantage of the weak
    or used force to get my way.
  Rather, I've tried to walk the high road with You.
    Though the path has sometimes been difficult,
      by Your power I have not slipped.

I have learned that You are a God who answers my prayers.
  You have showered me with Your love.
    You have delivered me from destruction.
      You have given my life meaning.
        You have sheltered me from the things that threaten.
      You have been my refuge and strength.

Please continue to watch over me.
  Be as diligent to preserve me as a man is to preserve his sight.
    Be as concerned with my welfare as a hen is for her chicks
      when she gathers them under her wings.

Everywhere I look I see dangers.
 I see people who have their minds set on violence.
  They have no compassion for the weak.
   They lie and kill without a pang of conscience.
 They boast of their immorality
  and pride themselves in their perversity.
   They are like predatory animals,
    always looking for ways to tear and maim.
 They lurk in the shadows
  and watch for any opportunity to harm.

I am sometimes filled with fear and dread.
 I feel alone and helpless,
  despondent,
   bewildered,
    weak,
     impotent,
      surrounded,
      betrayed.

O Lord, come to my rescue.
 Don't allow wrong to prevail.
  Protect me with Your might.
  Save me from my enemies.

You have taught me that appearances are deceiving.
 The wicked seem to be doing so well.
  They build up wealth,
   and live in big mansions,
    and control huge enterprises.
 On the surface they seem to be blessed
  with the best that life has to offer.
 They pass on their estates to their children and grandchildren.
  Nothing seems to be beyond their grasp.
   They indulge themselves and flaunt their success.

But their reward is in this life, not in the life to come.

You have taught me, O Lord, to be content in You.
  You have never abandoned those who trust in You.
    I have always had what I needed
      and You have blessed me with a spiritual inheritance
        to pass along to my children.

I want to take my stand for righteousness.
  I want to focus my eyes on You, O God.
    I want to direct my thoughts and ambitions toward You.
  I want to face each new day with You on my mind.
    I want to find my satisfaction not in what I own,
      O God, but in You who made me and own me.

I want to be like You.
  I want to learn the secret of Your ways
    so that all I do
      and all I am
        and all I possess
          glorify Your name
            and cause others to turn
              their eyes to You!

AMEN

PSALM 18

You alone are worthy of praise.
> You are a God who hears the prayers of the faithful.
>> You are my God and I will exalt You.

You bring me through times
> I do not think I can survive.

You rescue and redeem me.

In my direst need,
> You hear my prayers of desperation.

There are times when I feel strangled by my situation.
> I am swamped by my suffering,
>> drowned in my desolation.
>>> I feel suffocated,
>>>> tormented,
>>>>> defeated.

Death seems to be closing in on me.
> There seems no way out.
>> I am drained by despondency.

Then I lift up my voice and speak Your name.
> I cry out to You in the midst of my distress.
>> I call for help.
>> AND YOU HEAR.

It's as if I am in the midst of a violent thunderstorm.
> The earth seems to tremble beneath my feet.
>> Lightning flashes and thunder rumbles all about me.
> The world seems to be on fire,
>> the dark clouds, like smoke, roll and roil overhead.
>> A roaring wind bends all in its path.

Darkness descends, hail strikes with destructive, stinging force.
> Lightning streaks through the black clouds,
>> great bolts of terrifying, numbing power.
>>> Thunder crashes all about me.

Rain pelts down until the earth becomes like the sea.
> The wind screams in terrifying force.

Then You come into this scene of terror
  to calm the world and quiet my fears.
    You still the storm,
      and whisper words of peace.
    You reach down to me with reassurance,
      You take me in Your strong arms,
        and You draw me away from the dangers
          that threaten to overcome me.
    You rescue me from my adversities.
      You give me the strength I need to go on.

    You hush the storm and restore my hope and confidence.
      You bring me through the tempest
        with all its gloom and terror,
          to set my heart in a place of joy and beauty.
      You comfort me with the delight of Your loving care.

I am not always the person You want me to be.
  I am not always the person I want to be.
But I know that You are near me when I stand in righteousness.
  You bless me when I keep Your ways.
    You come to my aid
      when I come to You with a pure heart
        and with hands that are not given over to evil.
I desire to walk according to Your will.
  I want Your mind to be my mind as I make my decisions.
  I want my life to be free from sin and disobedience.

Help me to remember
  that You bring a clear conscience when I walk in purity.
    You stand by me, You forgive me,
      You are loving toward me.
But when I am conniving
  and seek my own benefit at the expense of others,
    You turn Your displeasure upon me.
When I am haughty and take credit
  for the good that comes my way,
    You bring me low.

O God, You give me insight into the meaning of life.
  You illuminate my going out and my coming in.
With Your help absolutely nothing is impossible for me.
  No enemy can overcome me.
      No obstacle can stand in my way.
      No circumstance can defeat me.

O God, I want to know You as You are.
  Your ways are wise;
      Your Word is flawless;
      Your providence is perfect.

Nothing in the whole of the universe compares with You.
  There is no other who loves and cares for me as You do.
      There is no other in whom I can put my hope and trust.
          There is no other who can give strength for my needs.
          There is no other who can bring
              balance and wholeness to my ways.
You give my life a lightness,
  a grace,
      a happiness,
          that I can scarcely describe.

You enable me to climb the mountains of my existence
  with the sure foot of a mountain deer.
      You enable me to reach heights of satisfaction
          and accomplishment that I can scarcely visualize.
  You make my path easy;
      You shield me from danger;
          You give me strength for my trials.

With Your help I can be free of despair.
  I can defeat my enemies.
      I can triumph over my troubles.
      I can put to flight my fears.
You absolutely discomfit my foes
  and annihilate my adversaries.

You deliver me from my difficulties and destroy my depression.
My oppressors can no longer touch me.
They are as helpless as dust.

Father, You are my victory.
You have saved me from malicious people.
You have given me a place in Your kingdom.
You have brought me blessings and significance.
You have given me a good name, influence, and meaning.

You are alive and well, O Lord!
You are here and active in my world.
You hear my prayers and deliver me from danger.
I will lift up Your name
and exalt You as my God and Savior.
You take my side in my conflicts;
You save me from my enemies;
You give my life purpose;
You rescue me from danger.

Therefore I will praise You with the whole of my heart, Lord.
I will sing praises to Your name.
I will exalt You wherever I am.
You have crowned my life with victory.
You have anointed me with Your lovingkindness.
I am a king, indeed!

O Lord, You are my strength and my song.
You are my firm foundation,
my place of defense,
my deliverer in times of trouble.
You protect me from adversity;
You surround me with Your might;
You give me strength and endurance;
You hold me up and keep me from danger.
Thank You, Lord!

AMEN

PSALM 19

Dear Lord,
  I thank You for the universe,
    that infinite expanse of created cosmos
      stretching farther than my eye can see
      or my telescope can discern
        or my mind can comprehend.

I see in the sky Your celestial billboard
  proclaiming Your limitless creativity
    and Your incomparable knowledge.
That heavenly proclamation of Your might
  extends throughout the whole earth.
No matter where we live,
  we cannot escape that magnificent testimony.
    It overarches all mankind,
      speaking a language understood by everyone.
    It cannot be ignored.

You chart the path of the sun.
  You gauge the inclination, revolution, and rotation of the earth.
    You give us warmth and light
      in both the physical and spiritual realms.
Your law is as perfect as Your heavens.
  Your testimonies are as true
    as the course of the celestial bodies.
Your statutes are pure,
  enlightening,
    righteous,
      true,
        everlasting.
You alone provide the way of positive change.
  You alone bring wisdom to my bewilderment.
    You alone bring joy to my aching heart.
      You alone bring sight to my blindness.
        You alone bring enduring cleansing to my soul.
        You alone are the source of righteousness.

Your statutes are more precious than gold.
Your guidance is sweeter than honey.
Your instructions for my life
are not only to be appreciated,
they are to be obeyed.
You reward me not for knowing Your will,
but for doing it.
Your statutes warn me,
expose my errors,
confront my secret sins,
and keep my heart from evil.
In keeping them, I experience freedom.

I want to live uprightly.
I want to break free from the grip of sin.
I want to be whole, clean, free, upright,
and, once again, innocent as a child.
You alone can bring this about in my life.
I want my words to please You.
I want my thoughts to honor You.
I want to be acceptable to You, O Lord.

Sometimes this all seems as impossible for me
as naming the stars of the sky,
but You supply my lack.
You are my hope,
my guide,
my enabler,
my rewarder,
and my redeemer.
The universe declares Your glory;
Your statutes proclaim Your authority.
Your cosmos broadcasts Your power;
Your laws publish Your love.
Help me to see....
Help me to listen....

AMEN

PSALM 20A

I thank You, Lord, that You are by my side in my troubles.
    You not only listen to my prayers,
        You answer them as well.
    You defend Your chosen ones.
        You send them strength and help
            in their times of greatest need.
    You remember and reward their faithfulness.

I will draw my joy and victory from You.
    Your flag will flutter over my fortress.
        Your name will I honor with my allegiance.
            Your Word will I trust.
                Your salvation will be my song.
You delight in giving me my fondest desires.
    You enable me to accomplish the purposes of my heart.
    You hear my prayers and grant my petitions.

I am often tempted to trust in myself,
    in my education,
        in my gift for words,
            in my wealth,
                in my personality,
                    in my ingenuity,
                        in my family reputation,
                          in my possessions,
                            and in my accomplishments.
But my hope must be in You, O Lord.
    I know that in You alone is my strength.
        In Your name is my victory.
        In Your power is my defense.
            In Your salvation is my deliverance.
I will trust in You, O Lord.
    I will boast of Your great name.
        I will stand firm in Your Word.
            I will rest secure on Your promises.
                I will triumph through Your might.

AMEN

PSALM 20B

Dear Lord, I pray for our national leaders.
　　There is so much pressure on them.
　　　　They have such a need for wisdom.
　　　　　　There are so many opportunities for compromise.
　　　　　　　　There are so many temptations lurking about them.
O Lord, may they be people who acknowledge Your sovereignty.
　　May they be people who conform their desires to Your will.
　　　　May they be people whose plans You can bless.
　　　　May they be people who wholly trust in You.

Protect them by Your power.
　　Lift them up in their distress.
　　　　Send them help in their times of need.
　　　　　　Protect them from the corruptions of power.
　　　　　　Reward their deeds of faith.
　　　　　　　　Prosper their initiatives of righteousness.
May they rule under the banner of Your justice.
　　May their desire be to honor Your name.
　　　　May their prime objective be to lead others to know You.

All weapons become obsolete.
　　There is always something new that is more destructive.
　　　　All economies decay,
　　　　　　all prosperity fades,
　　　　　　　　all international and institutional power erodes.
　　All of these things are useless for our defense
　　　　if You are not on our side.

Help us to know that in righteousness,
　　faith,
　　　　and trust in You
　　　　　　is our national strength.

O Lord, save our leaders!
　　Answer our prayers for their welfare—
　　　　and for ours.

AMEN

PSALM 21

How I rejoice in Your strength, O God.
  You keep me safe in all my affairs;
    You satisfy my every need;
      You grant the desires of my heart.
You treat me like a king,
  placing a golden crown on my head,
    bestowing glory and majesty,
      prolonging my days in splendor,
        and granting me untold blessings.
You fill me with gladness
  by Your provision and presence.

I trust in Your unfailing love;
  I stand firm before all that threatens me.
I fear nothing that may befall,
  and no one who sets himself against me.

Your mighty hand routs my enemies.
  They are consumed as by a mighty forest fire
    when they turn their wickedness against You—and me.
  They will not prosper for long
    for You will bring to nothing their evil plots
      and will ensnare them in their own evil schemes.
Your protection surrounds me in so many ways.

You dispel my worries
  and bring joy to my despair.
    You listen to my prayers
      and look out for my best interests.
You bring lasting success and prosperity of soul.

You crown my life with satisfaction,
  fill my days and nights with contentment,
    build my reputation,
      and give me joy
        through Your presence in my life.

You keep me from stumbling blindly through life.
  You give me purpose and direction.
    You point me toward eternal triumph
      and sustain me by Your stedfast love.
When I trust in You I need not fear.
  Nothing evil can overtake me.
    You guard the palace of my life
      with Your unfailing, loyal service.

Accept the praise, O God, that I lift up to You!

Thank You for expending Your great power on my behalf.
  Thank You for standing with me in Your strength.
    Thank You for caring,
      for loving,
        for providing,
          for defending,
          for leading,
            for blessing,
              for exalting,
                for gladdening,
                  for vindicating,
                    for saving.
    Thank You for life itself,
      for happiness,
        for honor,
          for success.

I want to praise You, O Lord,
  from the depths of my heart.
    I want to speak of Your greatness
      and call attention to Your ways.
I want to trust You in every aspect of my life.

I want to sing songs of Your might
  and write poems of Your greatness.
    I want to utter words that glorify You
      and do deeds that honor Your majesty.

You are eternally strong,
  gloriously mighty,
    wonderfully loving,
      magnificently kind,
        marvelously stedfast,
          overwhelmingly just,
            indescribably exalted.

I love
  and thank You,
    Lord.

AMEN

PSALM 22

O God, You seem so far from me at times.
  I just can't feel Your presence
    or see Your blessings in my life.
  It seems You are deaf to my prayers
    and that my groanings go unheeded.
  I call out to You both day and night,
    but You do not seem to respond.

Yet, I know that You are there!
  I know that You are King of all.
    I know that You have delivered the faithful in the past.
      You have come to the aid of those who trust in You.
But right now I feel so low.
  I feel rejected,
    inconsequential,
      despised,
        hollow,
          derided,
            insulted,
              mocked,
                ridiculed,
                  and forsaken
      in spite of my trust in You.

I am surrounded by unbelievers
  who mock both You and me.
    They ridicule my trust in You
      and dare You to come to my aid.
    They taunt me and make light of Your promises.
Yet I know that You have been with me
  from the very beginning of my life till now.
    You have always been my God,
      in my times of trouble as well as in my times of victory.
I've learned, from experience, to trust You implicitly.
  So in this time of trouble,
    I cast my lot with You and rely on You to deliver me.

My enemies encircle me.
   They call for my blood;
      they seek to devour me.
I am weak and racked with pain.
   My spirit is drained;
      my heart is broken.
I feel as if I am near death.
   I just can't hang on any longer.
      I feel as if I'm dying of thirst.
         I shake with weakness.
            I can hardly speak.

My foes are everywhere.
   They surround me like a pack of dogs.
      My body is bleeding;
         my frustration is evident to all;
            my weakness has become a spectacle.
   Around me are those who delight in my downfall.
   They would tear the clothes from my body.

But You, O Lord, are not as far away as I sometimes suppose.
   You come in Your strength to help Your suffering servant.
      You turn defeat into victory.
         You protect from encircling danger.
         You save from gathering enemies.
         You rescue from raging predators.

So I will praise You, O Lord.
   I will praise You in the congregation of the faithful.
      I will stand in awe of Your lovingkindness.
         I will honor You in my conversation.
         I will revere You in every thought.
For You do not forsake me in my suffering.
   You have not really turned a deaf ear to my entreaties.
   You have heard my cry for help.

I will assemble with others to exalt You.
   I will keep my promise to walk in Your Word.

You bring satisfaction and fullness;
　You bring lasting joy and gladness.
The whole earth will come to know You.
　All nations will ultimately acknowledge You as God.
You are King over all,
　the sovereign Lord of all.

Rich and poor will all see death,
　and they will all acknowledge You
　　as ruler and judge.
The story of Your righteousness
　will be proclaimed for all time.
　　The glory of Your deeds
　　　will be recounted with wonder and adoration.

Father, in this period of depression
　You have allowed me
　　to enter into the experience
　　　of Jesus on the cross.
He cried out in His agony just as I cry out to You.
　It seemed as if You had forsaken Him
　　as He hung there.
　　　He was mocked,
　　　　insulted,
　　　　　ridiculed,
　　　　　　and tormented by His enemies.
His body was wrenched
　by the cruelty of that instrument of death.
　　He suffered excruciating physical pain.
　　　His hands and feet were pierced by nails.
　　　　His clothing was taken from him and distributed by lot.
　　　　He died a cruel death for my sins.

Yet, He rose again!
　You restored Him to life and vitality.
　　You lifted Him up from the grave to the throne of glory.
Now people from all nations can call Him King
　and acknowledge His rule in their lives.

You bring satisfaction and fullness;
  You bring lasting joy and gladness.
The whole earth stands in awe of Jesus,
  crucified for our sins,
    and victorious over death.

AMEN

PSALM 23

My life is in Your hands, O Shepherd of my soul.
  You fill my life with succulence,
    You lead me in the paths of peace.
  You bring rest to my weariness and hope to my failures.
    You lift me up when I am weak;
      You protect me when I am vulnerable.
  You watch out for the dangers that threaten me;
    You always have my best interests in mind.
  You are constantly by my side,
    ready to give me rest and comfort.
  You anoint my head with healing,
    and refresh my spirit with newness.

I know that because of You
  my days are filled with goodness,
    tranquillity,
      prosperity,
        quietness,
          abundance,
            contemplation,
            safety,
              renewal,
                direction,
                  honor,
                    courage,
                      companionship,
                      comfort,
                        provision,
                          healing,
                            refreshment,
                              mercy,
                                hope.
I know that I dwell under Your loving, watchful eye
  as long as I live,
    and that I am destined
      for the eternal sanctuary of Your presence forever.

                                        AMEN

PSALM 24

Yours is the earth
  and all things in it, O Lord—
    the mist-covered mountains,
      the surging seas,
        the teeming cities,
          the quiet towns,
            the shifting deserts,
              the mirrored lakes,
                the gurgling streams,
                  the radiant wild flowers,
                    the whispering wheat fields,
                      the refreshing forests,
                        the lush meadows,
    the soaring eagles,
      the chirping crickets,
        the playful dolphins,
          the mighty blue whales,
            the shimmering seals,
              the belligerent bears,
                the graceful gazelles,
                  the bouncing kangaroos,
                    the sauntering emus,
                      the wobbling wombats,
                        the graceful cranes,
    the flapping storks,
      the quick alligators,
        the plodding camels,
          the lumbering hippos,
            the clinging ladybugs,
              the radiant butterflies,
                the observant aborigine,
                  the careful scholar,
                    the resourceful Bedouin,
                      the hopeful politician,
                        the skilled laborer,
                          the cuddly baby,

the farsighted administrator,
the independent highlander,
the resourceful technician
the displaced refugee,
the struggling farmer,
the faithful parent,
the weary student,
the hopeless misfit,
the failed bumbler,
the disillusioned idealist,
the bitter criminal,
the lost infidel,
All the world is Yours,
and all things in it.
You uphold the earth.
You keep it rotating on its axis.
You keep it spinning in the heavens.
You set its angle of inclination,
You regulate its atmosphere,
and You control its climate.

Your creative, upholding power
is seen everywhere,
for You are a God of wonder and might.

What do you want of me—
I, who am such a small, insignificant part
of this magnificent creation?
What will please You most?

You desire that I keep my hands and mind from evil,
that I forsake selfish, grasping ways,
that I live and labor in purity,
and that I walk in justice, mercy, and truth.

You want of me a clean heart—
pure motives,
consistent faith,

    trusting deeds,
     righteous thoughts,
      truthful utterance,
       obedient lifestyle,
        undiluted praise,
         unfeigned humility,
          and loving service.

You, the Author of all salvation
 and the Source of all righteousness,
  are the Giver of rich blessing
   to those who
    commit their ways to You.

You desire to take residence in my life, O Lord.
 Help me to throw open the gates of my heart to You.
 Help me to open the doors of my defenses,
  and breach the walls of my willfulness,
   so that You can take full possession of me.

You are my King, strong and mighty,
 incomparable in Your riches,
  unfailing in Your righteousness,
   consistent in Your holiness,
    equipped for any test,
     undismayed by any eventuality,
      constant in Your love.

Thank You, O glorious Sovereign,
 for making me Your palace,
  for sending forth Your righteous decrees through me,
   for doing battle with evil alongside me,
    for using me to reach the lost.

Displace the pretenders to Your throne,
 so that I may magnify Your name alone,
  forever and ever.

Dwell in me, O Lord,
  that my hands and feet may do Your work,
    that my thoughts may dwell on Your greatness,
      that my lips may sing Your praises,
        that my heart may meditate on Your decrees.

May I be as filled with Your presence in my small inner world,
  as is my external world,
    the universe of Your creation.
May I be as controlled by Your will
  as is the spinning world on which I dwell.
May I know Your blessings of righteousness and salvation.
  May I seek You with all my heart, soul, and mind.
May I worship You with pure thoughts, words, and deeds.
  May my refuge and joy be in You.

Make a triumphal entry into my life, O Lord.
  I throw open the gates and doors of my innermost citadel.
Take up Your residence in me.
  Rule from the throne of my heart.
    Extend the joys of Your kingdom through me.

Live in me, King of Glory,
  Lord of Hosts,
    strong and mighty to save!

AMEN

PSALM 25

O God, You are my constant preoccupation.
  You are the object of my love,
    the center of my trust.
You are the source of my hope,
  the protector of my good name,
    the champion of my cause,
      the vindicator of my honor,
        the shelter of my soul,
          the security of my being.
  I need not worry,
    for You are watchful
      and will protect me from the snares of the treacherous.
Help me to learn how to live in wisdom.
  Show me Your ways.
    Lead me down the right paths.
      Guide me in Your truth.
        Teach me Your will.
You alone are my hope.
  You alone are my God and my Savior.

Please, O Lord, forgive the sins of my past,
  my reckless disregard for things eternal,
    my rebelliousness and self-will.
  Forgive my futile ambitions,
    my desire for the approval of men more than
      my desire for Your approval,
    my timidity in proclaiming Your greatness,
      my pride and arrogance,
        my disobedience,
          my sensuality,
            my preoccupation with my pleasure,
              my sins of the mind and body,
                my lack of godly compassion,
                  my callousness to the needs of others,
                    my childish demands,
                      my wasted opportunities.

Help me to grow up.
Help me to demonstrate Your love and goodness
in every relationship of my life.
Help me to honor Your statutes
and imitate Your nature
in the ordinary experiences of each day.

O Father, don't treat me as I deserve.
Forgive me for the waywardness of my past.
Liberate me from the frustration and futility
of the mistakes that clog the memory banks of my mind.
Remove my guilt.
Free me from the despair of my failures.
Purge me from the pain of my past.
Cleanse me.
Look on me through Your eyes of love,
O God of goodness,
and free me from guilt and fear.

O Lord, You alone are perfectly good and upright,
Yet, You have not remained aloof and far off.
You have reached down to sinful man
and given him instruction in Your ways.
You show grace to the humble
and have revealed Your will
through the Scriptures
so that we may know that
You are loving and faithful.

I have no merit
that You should shower me with Your kindness.
I can only ask that You forgive me
on the basis of Your nature, not mine.

I know that I am unworthy of Your concern.
I know that my sins are multitudinous
and that my iniquities are horrible,
yet I ask Your forgiveness and blessing.

Lord, I want to honor You with my life.
  Instruct me in the way You have chosen for me.
    Keep my life from futility and emptiness.
      Shower me with Your richness.
        Give me an inheritance that goes on
          from generation to generation
            in my posterity of faith.

Make known Your will to me.
  Reveal Your purposes.
    Commune as a friend with me.
      Allow me to enter into Your confidences.
        Draw me close to Your heart.
          Make known to me Your principles of life.
          Live in and through me.
You know me better than I know myself.
  Help me to keep my eyes focused on You,
    for You alone can dispel the blindness of my life.
      You alone know where the pitfalls are
        that lie in wait to harm me.

I know that I can put my trust in You,
  for You are gracious and mighty.
    When I feel alone and tormented,
      depressed and despondent,
        defeated and broken,
          helpless and hopeless,
    You come to my rescue.
  When I strike out,
    or mess up,
      or run aground,
        or miss the boat,
  You treat me with respect and compassion.
  When I feel so burdened down I can hardly go on,
    You reach out to me with deliverance
      and put together again
        the fractured pieces of my life.

You are my deliverance.
You are my strength.
You are my refuge.
You are my fortress
and hiding place.
My life is in Your hands, O Lord.
You are my lifeboat,
my fire extinguisher,
my emergency brake,
my smoke alarm,
my parachute,
my safety belt.

I thank You that You can remove
the awful consequences of sin.
You bring me freedom from all the enemies of my soul.
You guard my life
and rescue me from danger.

Come to my aid, O Father,
in my times of need.
Keep me from danger
and preserve me from destruction.
I put my hope in You, O Lord,
for You alone are right and true.

What I desire for myself, O God,
I also desire for my nation.
Please keep it on the true path, O Lord.

AMEN

PSALM 26

O Lord, I come before You as one who seeks
  to walk the path of holiness.
    I would stand in innocence before You.
I would trust You with my whole heart.
  I would rely on You for my salvation.
    I would lean upon You for my strength.
      I would be resolute in doing what is right in Your eyes.

Help me to keep my footing
  as I walk through life.
    Help me to keep my desires in check
      and my thoughts in control.
Help me to walk in Your truth
  and not turn away toward disobedience.
    Don't let me slide into rebellion
      or fall into evil.

You know my heart and mind.
  Help me to root out all that is not of You.
    Make known to me Your judgment.
      Expose my wayward thoughts and evil desires.
Call me to account that I may be purified by Your instruction.
  Examine me that I may learn Your standards.
    Help me to recognize Your sovereignty in my decisions.
    Help me to conform my desires to Your will
      and my designs to Your way.

I know that You are a constant and sure guide.
  You do not lead me in the way of disaster.
    You do not abandon me when the path becomes difficult.
      You do not lead me into the swamps of despair
        or the deserts of hopelessness.
  You lead me with love
    and with consideration for my frail humanity.
  You are dependable, wise, and constant.
    I need not fear for my life when I follow Your leading.

Help me to keep my eyes focused on Your lovingkindness
    and my heart fixed on Your truth.
      Help me to watch my associations
        so that I do not become friends with wickedness.
Help me to be careful of the people I allow to influence my life.

Keep me from compromising
    and from seeking the acceptance of evildoers.
      Help me to be pure in my business ethics
        and circumspect in the choice of my closest friends.
    Keep my mouth from conversations that condone evil.
    Make me uncomfortable
      in the company of those who slander You.
Help me to stand firmly for what is right
    rather than to settle amiably for what is expedient.

Lord, I am most at home
    when I come into a place
      where You are worshiped.
        I love to think upon Your glory
          and to contemplate Your mighty acts in history.
  I desire to enter Your sanctuary with a pure heart.
    I look forward to coming before You
      with my sacrifice of praise.
  To stand before You without guilt or hypocrisy
    is my greatest delight.
With clean hands and heart,
    I want to present my life as a sacrifice to You.
      It thrills me to hear Your great deeds recounted.
        It lifts up my spirit to sing hymns of thanks to You.
    It warms me to be with Your people
      and to know Your blessing.

I do not want to live a life of disobedience.
    I do not desire to be grouped with sinners.
      I do not want to associate comfortably with the ungodly.
        I do not want to be among those that murder and steal.
        I do not want to live outside Your blessing.

I want to do right
  so that I can experience
    Your mercy and salvation.
I want to walk in integrity.
  I want to worship You in joyful assembly.
    I want my words
      and my life
        to bless Your name.

AMEN

PSALM 27

You, O Lord, are my light and my salvation.
  You are my refuge and my strength.
    No evil can befall me.
      No foe can overcome.
        No disaster overtake.
  Though I am surrounded by dangers,
    nothing really frightens me.
        Though I am engulfed by uncertainty,
          I am confident in Your presence.

I have one desire—
  that I may live victoriously with You
    all the days of my life.
I want my eyes to look upon Your glory.
  I want my steps to take me into Your presence.
    I want to rest securely in Your holy dwelling place.
You shelter me from the sun and the storm;
  You protect me from adversity;
    You lift me toward the high places,
      where I look down on my enemies
        from a vantage point of strength and security.

I want to sing Your praises, Lord.
  I want to shout for joy.
    I want to make music of adoration.
Hear me when I pray, O God.
  Forgive me and heed my requests.
    I want to seek Your approval.
      I want to know Your presence.
        I want to experience Your approval.

Please, Lord, do not turn away from me.
  Don't be angry at my waywardness.
    You are my constant help.
      Stay with me, O Lord.
        Accept my praise and love.

You are faithful.
  Though everyone else in the world
    deserts me and abandons me,
      You still hold me and draw me to You.

Help me to know You as You are, O Lord.
  Keep me on the straight and narrow path.
    Don't let me depart from Your will.
Don't let the enemies of my soul prevail.
  Don't let falsehood and violence overpower me.

There is much I don't know,
  but I am confident of this one thing—
    I can trust my present and my future to You, O Lord.
You will bless me with long and satisfying life.
  I will look expectantly
    for what You will bring about, O Lord.
      I will wait patiently for Your will to be done.

Make me strong,
  brave,
    stouthearted,
      courageous,
        and faithful.

AMEN

PSALM 28

O Lord, whose strength is my security,
hear my prayer.
Life to me
is communion with You.
If you don't hear my petitions,
I might as well be dead.
You stand with me in my need;
You reach out to me in mercy;
You inhabit my praise.

Father, I want to live before You in truth.
I don't want to be counted among the wicked.
I don't want to be at ease with those who do evil.
I don't want to be hypocritical—
appearing to be something that I am not,
pretending to be friendly to others
while I secretly stab them in the back,
speaking outward words of kindness
while inwardly thinking thoughts of animosity.

Father, don't let evildoers go unpunished.
Give them the justice they deserve.
Let their wicked deeds return on their own heads.
Disestablish,
undermine,
destroy,
bring down
all those who disregard You
and Your mighty works.

Lord, You are the object of my praise.
You listen to my prayers
and respond in mercy to my entreaties.
You are my strength and my defender.
When I put my trust in You,
I always find the help I need.

You are my source of joy and gladness.
   I thank You for all Your goodness.
      I lift up to You the song of a grateful heart.
You are my strong defender,
   my wall of deliverance,
      and my fortress of salvation.

I thank You for anointing me with Your loving concern.
   I thank You for Your promise of a glorious legacy.
      I bless Your name for Your watchcare.
You look after me like a shepherd cares for his flock.
   You carry me like a young lamb.
      I am protected,
         honored,
            valued,
               cared for,
                  loved.

You respond to my cry for help;
   You protect me from trouble;
      You provide strength and deliverance;
         You fill my life with the joy of my salvation.

Your love is unbounded,
   eternal,
      ever watchful,
         unlimited,
            everlasting.

Thank You, Lord!

AMEN

PSALM 29

I want to join the celestial beings
  in speaking of Your glory and power, O Lord.
    I want to give to You
      the praise that You alone deserve.

Your name is magnificent.
  Your character is unmatched.
    Your holiness is unsullied.
      Your nature is resplendent.

I hear Your voice in the storm, O Lord.
  It thunders to the ends of the sea in the mighty gale.
    It claps from the heavens in the lightning flash.
Nature speaks of Your power and majesty.
  You splinter the mightiest forest with Your whisper.
    You shake the soaring mountains with Your words.
      Your voice booms through lightning
        that severs the night sky with earsplitting power.
  Your voice sends tremors through the desert
    and splits open great fissures in the earth.
  It sends tornadoes twisting through forests,
    destroying all that lies in their paths.

Everything in this world speaks Your glory, O Lord.
  You hold the mighty waters in their places.
    You sit high above the stratosphere,
      observing,
        sustaining,
          ordering,
            ruling.
    You reign supreme,
      everlasting,
        secure,
          almighty,
            strong,
              true.

But You, who show Your strength in the mountain storm
   and in the desert earthquake,
      are not unmindful of the needs
        of Your people.
You grant us strength in our times of need.
   You shower us with the blessing of peace.
      You quiet our storms with the word of Your power.
      You hush our anxieties
        and surround us with Your love.

You give to us from Your unlimited resources.
   You shelter us from catastrophe.
      You come to our aid when we are weak.
      You give us power to overcome our difficulties.

Father, what a great and wonderful God You are!
   I see You in all that is.
      I worship You with my whole heart.
      I thank You for Your blessings.
      I walk in Your peace.

Father, what a great and wonderful God You are!

AMEN

PSALM 30

I will lift up my praise to You, O Lord,
 for You have lifted me up from the depths
  and made me to stand in confidence and strength.

When I call upon You for help,
 You listen and respond.
  You bind up my wounds
   and mend the brokenness of my life.
 You protect me from my enemies
  and keep me from the pit of despair
   and the darkness of death.
I will join the saints, both living and dead,
 in a glad song of praise to Your holy name.

There are times when I experience Your discipline,
 but by comparison to Your favor,
  it is but a momentary testing.
 Your loving care will follow me all my life.
  You watch over me through the night
   and dispel my darkness with the light of joy.

As long as I turn my face toward You
 I experience strength and stability.
  You have given me a firm foundation,
   a place to stand,
    a secure handhold.
 When I walk in Your approval
  I am never defeated.
   But when I forsake You,
    I am overthrown.

Lord, I have wept before You
 and You have heard my prayers.
  You are the source of mercy.
   You are the supplier of help.
    You give my life meaning.

I want to praise You with all the breath life gives me,
  for You animate the dust from which I am formed
    with Your Holy Spirit.
  I must honor You while life and breath are in me,
    for I can never know when my earthly end will come.
  I must proclaim Your faithfulness and speak of Your glory
    for that is the purpose for which I have been given life.

Hear me, O Lord.
  Help me, O Lord.
    Heal me, O Lord.

You have turned me from sorrow to joy.
  I feel like singing and dancing.
    You have resuscitated my spirit
      and lifted the sackcloth of sorrow from my body.
        You have given me a new song
          and a new voice to sing it.

O Lord my God,
  I can never worship You enough.
    I want to do homage to Your name forever.

I will lift up my praise to You, O Lord,
  for You have lifted me up from the depths
    and made me to stand in confidence and strength!
  My exuberance cannot be stifled.

I must sing,
  shout,
    and loudly proclaim
      that You are my God.
I will praise You with thanksgiving
  forever and ever!

AMEN

PSALM 31

Lord, it seems as if I pray most ardently in times of trouble.
  It's then that I realize how weak I truly am
    and how much I must depend upon You.

Lord, this is one of those times.
  I know that You never let me down.
    You never leave me exposed and defenseless
      to face my troubles alone.
    You always know and do what is right,
      so I ask You to come to my aid in my present difficulties.

Please, Lord, listen to my prayers,
  these words of trust and praise
    that pour out from my anguish of soul
      and my desire to know Your deliverance.

O Lord, I can't hold on much longer.
  I need Your help right now.
    I'm in a situation that needs a speedy resolution.
      I ask You to give ear to my entreaty
        and to protect me from the foes that encircle me.

You are my refuge,
  my strong foundation,
    my high place of certainty,
      my vantage point of hope.
You surround me with Your mighty fortification,
  You defend me with Your great might,
    You save me from the designs of my destroyers.

O Holy Father, Your name is everything to me.
  In Your name I live each day of my life.
    I seek to follow Your leading;
      I seek to walk in Your ways.
    Please, Lord, don't let anything that befalls me
      cause me to bring dishonor to Your reputation.

All who know me know that I've tried to trust faithfully in You.
  If I fall and fail in my present problems,
    Your name will be dishonored as well as mine.
  Others will speak ill of Your providence and power.
    They will make light of faith and trust
      and laugh at Your goodness and love.
Father, please don't let that happen.
  Deliver me from the hidden dangers
    that lie secretly in wait to do me harm.
      In my limitations I cannot know them,
        but all things are known to You.
          Walk by my side and guide my footsteps
            through the minefields of this time.
  Take my hand and lead me like a child
    where You would have me go.
  You are my eyes and ears
    and my strength for the future.
      You have taken control of my life
        and brought me back from destruction.
      Guide me in the path of triumph and gladness.

I've tried to turn my back on falsehood and empty religion.
  I've tried to make You truly God of my life.
    I've sought to rid myself of idols and false allegiances.
      I've kept clear of profane and immoral people
        who would entice me with vanity and sin.

With my whole heart, O Lord, I do trust You.
  You are my source of joy and gladness.
    You have demonstrated Your stedfast love and mercy
      wherever my footfall has gone.
  You have been very close to me in my troubles.
    You have not allowed my enemies to prevail.
      You have directed my path in the way of victory.
      You have cut a wide swath for me through the
        jungles of my adversity.

Lord, I need Your help just now.
  Look on me with mercy and kindness.

I can't seem to see anything but my turmoil.
My eyes are blinded with tears;
my body aches with fear;
my soul is in the pit of despair.
I seem to spend all my time in sorrow.
My days and nights are filled
with groaning of mind and spirit.
I feel like a wet blanket,
a spineless jellyfish,
a lost cause.

I know that there is sin in my life.
I know that when I transgress Your will
such difficult times inevitably come.
I know that when I am at war with You
I have turmoil and strife within my own heart
and hostility with those who surround me.
I am alienated from my friends
and am abandoned by those upon whom I have come to rely
for encouragement and consolation.
I am ignored and forsaken
and thrown away like a burned out lightbulb.
I might as well be dead
so far as my acquaintances are concerned.
Not only my friends forsake me,
but my enemies join in the carnage.
They speak ill of me at every opportunity;
they plot my downfall;
they rejoice in my defeat.
My life seems to be crumbling;
my world is disintegrating around me.

But, in the midst of even this dire situation,
I know You are my God
and I can put my trust in You!

My future is in Your hands, O God.
Keep me safe through this troubled time.
Don't let me fall before my foes.

Look on me with favor.
   Save me by Your mercy.
      Don't rain ridicule and shame down on my head
         as the fallout of this experience.
   Rather, bring disgrace on the heads of those
      who oppose You,
         and spread their lies,
            belittling what is right.

Your goodness is great, O God.
   I know I can rely on You.
      In this threatening situation You will bring a resolution
         that turns my weariness to strength
            and my weeping to shouts of joy.
      You are faithful to those who fear You.
         You are good to those who trust in You.
      You keep them from danger;
         You protect them from foes;
            You cover them with Your panoply of love;
            You protect their names from slander.

Blessed be Your name, O Lord!
   It is in times like this
      that I come to appreciate You best.
   In the midst of difficulties
      I see most graphically my need for You.
   Like a city that has successfully resisted an enemy,
      I breathe the air of freedom more thankfully
         when I realize
            that the seige towers have been taken away.

Sometimes I am quick to give up.
   I think that You are unconcerned with my difficulty.
      I act as if You have no interest in my downfall.

But I have learned that this is never really the case.
   You *do* have ears for my prayers.
      You *do* listen to my anguished cries.

You *do* take an interest in the affairs of the faithful.
You *do* bring down the pretensions of the wicked.
You *do* look on Your sanctified ones with love.

Therefore, I know that I can face this day with courage, O Lord.
You will provide the strength I need.
You will gladden my thoughts with hope.
You will bring the joy of a new day.

AMEN

PSALM 32

O Lord, I rejoice in the fact that my sins are forgiven.
  You have blotted out my transgression
    and covered my iniquity.
  You have put my life together.
    You have delivered me from the punishment
      that is my due.
  You have brought happiness
    and saved me from defilement.

When I tried to resist You,
  my life was destitute and drained.
    When I failed to confess my guilt,
      my life became one large ache.
Your displeasure was evident in all that I did
  and everything I touched turned to dust.

But when I confessed my sin to You,
  when I owned up to my disobedience,
    when I acknowledged my evasions,
      my rationalizations,
        and my excuses,
    then You forgave me of my guilt
      and washed away my iniquity.

It is all too wonderful to understand!
  I desire Your forgiveness and come seeking Your approval.
    Help me to be diligent in prayer while I have breath
      and life to express my gratitude to You.
    I thank You for lifting me up
      above the murky and threatening waters of danger
        and setting me on the high ground of Your grace.
  You are my refuge,
    my sanctuary,
      my fortress.
        I need not fear for You surround me
          with songs of deliverance.

O Lord, I thank You for Your instruction,
   Your infallible teaching about the way of life.
      Thank You for guiding me with Your counsel
         and Your clear-eyed foresight.
I thank You that You do not treat me like a dumb animal.
   You do not lead me about with a bit and bridle.
      You respect my individuality,
         my freedom,
            my faith,
               my personal identity.
You do not overpower me,
   or override my will with Your desires for me.
      You reach out to me with love and respect,
         not coercion and compulsion.

The wicked are always in the midst
   of one kind of trouble or another.
      But when I trust in You
         things seem to fall into place,
            blessings pour in upon me,
               and my life is filled with untold satisfaction.
      You surround me with Your mercy;
         You fill my life with gladness;
            You cleanse my conscience.

I rejoice in You, O Lord.
   I shout for joy;
      I lift my heart in glad adoration.

AMEN

PSALM 33

Lord, it is a joyful thing to make music of praise to You.
It is wonderful to sing songs of adoration with the saints.
My heart is lifted up
when I hear You praised on stringed instruments.
I love to compose new songs of spontaneous joy,
and shout my exuberant praise to Your holy name.

Thank You for giving vibrating strings
the ability to create
beautiful melodies and chords of adoration.
Thank You for creating my vocal chords
with the ability to express
words of worship and appreciation.
Give me skill to sing and play,
so that my music and words may be lifted up to You
as expressions of creative ingenuity
and offerings of skillful excellence.

Lord, You are so faithful in all Your works!
Your Word guides me in truth and righteousness.
You look with approval on justice and goodness.
Your love fills the whole earth.

Your word is powerful.
It formed the heavens,
flung out the stars,
and hollowed the seas.
You spoke the world into existence;
You uphold the whole earth
by the word of Your power.
Let all of creation bow down before You.
Let every human being on the face of the earth
acknowledge Your sovereignty,
and realize that no one
and no thing
can stand in the way of Your will.

If You choose,
    You can overthrow nations and bring down kings,
      unseat presidents, defeat mighty armies,
        and neutralize complex war machines.
    You can level the exalted,
      destroy the proud, and frustrate the powerful.

Your will is firm and consistent.
    You bring to pass the desires of Your heart.
      You are never thwarted in Your plans,
        never turned away from Your purpose.

Lord, how our nation needs You!
    We need the blessing that comes from true worship.
      We crave the comfort of Your approval.

I know, O Lord, that nothing we do escapes Your notice.
    You observe our plans,
      our plots,
        our programs,
          our goals,
            our philosophies,
              our intrigues,
              our values,
                our priorities,
                our deeds,
                  and our motives.

It isn't atomic stockpiles
    that will save our nation from destruction.
      It isn't intercontinental missiles,
        tanks, aircraft carriers, atomic submarines,
        radar installations, or B-1 bombers
          that will assure
            our continuation and prosperity.

Such instruments of war are powerless to save.
    They are a vain hope for a nation
      whose heart is not committed to You.

But You do look with favor
on those who put You first in their lives,
who respect Your Word,
and who seek to do Your will.
You protect those who put their confidence and hope
in Your constant love.
You deliver those
who trust You for their very lives.
You rescue from want those
who commit their destinies to Your faithful care.

Lord, make me that kind of person!
Help me to put my trust wholly in You.
Be my shield and sustainer.
Fill my life with the joy of Your presence.
Teach me to believe You with all my heart.
Help me to put my hope for the future in You.
Overshadow me with Your love!

Lord, You are so faithful in all Your works!
Your Word guides me in truth and righteousness.
You look with approval on justice and goodness.
Your love fills the whole earth.
Let all of creation bow down before You.
Let every human being on the face of the earth
acknowledge Your sovereignty!

AMEN

PSALM 34

Lord, help me to develop an attitude of prayer.
  Help me to think constantly of You,
    communicating with You,
      depending on You,
        walking with You.
  Help me to learn how to praise You as I ought.
    Give me a diligence for spiritual discipline.
      Teach me how to be Your person on this earth.

My life is Your dwelling place.
  You are my confidence,
    my strength,
      and my hope.
  You restore the brokenness of my life
    and transform my afflictions into joy.
  My worth is derived from my relationship with You.
    My happiness is bound up in homage of Your name.

Help me to be a catalyst of praise,
  an instigator of adoration,
    a motivator of thanksgiving,
      so that all who come in contact with my life
        may see the wonder of Your glory reflected in me.

I join today, O Lord,
  the great company of men and women
    who have learned the secret of dependence on You.
I glorify Your name in the fellowship of the faithful.
  It is good to praise You and glorify Your name.

So many times in the past I have turned to You in my need.
  You have heard my prayers and answered me.
You have not always done precisely what I had in mind.
  You have not always worked according to my timetable.
    You have often surprised me
      with Your solutions to my problems.

But You have always brought me through
   the things that overwhelmed me.
      You have always looked after my needs.
You have always delivered me from fear and desperation.
     You have always come to my rescue with renewal and hope.
      You have lifted up my countenance.
        You have brought a smile to my lips.
         You have smoothed the furrows of my brow.
        You have relaxed my tension,
          removed my stress, eased my pain.

Your love surrounds me with good.
   Your angels encircle me with Your might.
     Your watchcare never slumbers nor forsakes.
I am secure with You
   even when I am surrounded by troubles.

What a wonderful thing prayer is!
   Through it You are available to me.
     You treat me like a king.
       You surround me with Your bodyguard
       and watch after my every need.
         You deliver me from everything
          that threatens my security.

O Lord, You are so good!
   I have tasted Your love,
     and I know that it satisfies as nothing else
      in the whole of creation.
   Help me to develop an appetite for You.
    Help me to experience Your goodness.
     Help me to hide myself in You.
       Help me to recognize Your authority in my life.

When I fear You,
   I need not fear anything else.
    You supply my every need.
     I lack nothing when I walk in Your ways.

I need not fear for my reputation,
  my material needs,
    my future,
      my relationships,
        my success,
          my salvation,
            my food,
              my shelter,
                or my safety
      when I put my trust in You.

I have no anxieties
  when I am in tune with You.
    You know exactly what I need
      and You supply it from Your abundance.
      When I seek You,
        I find meaning and purpose in my life.
        I find joy,
          fulfillment,
            contentment,
              and happiness.

Lord, help me to know what it is to fear You.
  I know that it doesn't mean that I am to cower
    before You in anguished terror,
      for You are a loving Father who cares for me.
  Yet, I need to know how to relate to You as I ought.

Teach me, O Father, a proper attitude toward You.

I know You want to take control of my mouth.
  You want my lips to speak truth and righteousness.
    You want me to shun self-serving falsehood.
      You want me to deal honestly with my fellowmen.
That is not always easy for me, Father.
  I am so prone to bend the truth to my advantage.
    It is such a temptation
      for me to tell less than the whole truth.

I know, too, that You want to take control of my lifestyle.
  You want me to be able to discern good from evil.
    And You want me to turn away from evil.
That, too, is sometimes so difficult for me.
  I'm surrounded by immorality.
    It leers at me from my television set.
      It beckons me from my magazines.
        It entices me in my books.
It isn't very popular these days to be righteous.
  A lot of people can't understand it
    when I take a stand on moral issues.
Yet I know that You want me to turn my thoughts
  and actions away from evil.
    You want me to do good.
You want me to walk among men and women in peace.
  You have called me to walk the path of forgiveness
    rather than revenge.

I know that if I do these things I will be happy.
  I will be spared the diseases of discontent
    and the maladies of bitterness.
  You will give me a long and full life.
    I may not be successful in the eyes of the world,
      but I will experience the best that life can offer.
        I will know peace and contentment.
O Lord, help me to be like You.

Thank You, Lord, for being sensitive to my needs,
  for watching after my well-being.
I know that when I obey You and listen to Your Word
  You are always open to my entreaties.
Yet when I turn away to wickedness,
  You must turn against me as well.
    My life becomes a mess
      and I go down to ignominious defeat.
    Everything turns to dust,
      and contentment is replaced with futility.

Thank You, Lord, for the promises You have made to the righteous.
   You have committed Yourself to respond to their prayers.
   You have promised Your deliverance.
     You will bind up their wounds,
      mend their broken hearts,
       and restore their shattered spirits.

I know, Lord, that You have not promised a trouble-free life.
   You do not put a protective bubble around Your saints.
    You do not shield them from every conflict
     or whisk them away from every difficulty.
  Rather, You come to their aid in the midst of their troubles.
   You lead them through the dark valleys.
    You give them courage in the midst of hardship.
     You refine them by means of the tests of their lives.
 You stand with the righteous,
   leading them when they cannot see,
     giving them endurance when they want to give up,
      helping them when they cannot help themselves.

I don't need to fear evil people so long as I fear You.
  I don't need to fear circumstances so long as I fear You.
   I don't need to fear disappointment and failure
    so long as I fear You.
 For I can rely on You to take my part
   whatever the foe, whatever the fear, whatever the failure.

Lord, I want to be the kind of servant You can bless in this way.
  Help me to love righteousness and pursue it with all my heart.
   Help me to experience, today, the freedom of Your friendship.
Thank You for freeing me from the fear of Your condemnation.
  I know that I deserve Your wrath, not Your kindness.
Thank You for the precious promises of Your Word,
  the unlimited resources of prayer,
    the unfathomable riches of Your love.
     O God, You are so good!
      Help me to know You as I ought.

AMEN

PSALM 35

Lord, things are not going well.
    Please take up my cause and contend for me.
        Stand with me in this fight.
            Come to my aid in this present difficulty.
                Arise and take up arms on my behalf.
                    Assure me that You are by my side in this conflict.
                        Deliver me from those who seek my downfall.
I feel as if I'm surrounded by hostile forces
    bent on taking away my life,
        plotting my ruin,
            setting traps for me at every turn,
                suborning witnesses against me,
                    eagerly anticipating my failure,
                        mocking my every deed,
                            hating me without cause,
                                spreading lies about my motives and actions.

Father, don't let them succeed in their evil plans.
    Bring shame and disgrace upon them.
        Thwart their well-laid plots.
            Divide and conquer them.
Scatter them like chaff before the wind of Your might.
    Darken their way.
        Make their path insecure.
Pursue them with Your avenging angel.
    Entangle them in their own snares.
        Ruin them by their own hand.
            Put them to shame and confusion.
                Cover them with disgrace.
                    Rescue me from their malicious lies.
                        Vindicate me in Your righteousness.
Then my joy will be overflowing!
    The wonder of my salvation will be very evident.
        My whole being will proclaim Your deliverance.
            I will know Your holiness
                and speak from experience of Your salvation.

I marvel at Your ways.
   I am confident of Your compassion.
      I know that You are a God who comes to the aid of the needy
         and who protects the weak and the helpless.

You know how bad things have become!
   I'm constantly under attack for one thing or another.
      I'm continually being accused and questioned.
         I try to return good for evil.
            I know that that is the way of Christ.
   When my foes have problems
      I do my best to be of help.
         I try to act in humility
            and to be compassionate in their times of distress.
   I pray for them earnestly.
      I try to treat them as close friends or relatives.

Yet, they return hatred for my concern.
   They delight when they see me stumble.
      They rejoice when I am besieged by secret plotters.
   They take glee when my name is slandered undeservedly.
      They miss no opportunity to display their contempt for me.

Lord, I do not know how long I can hold on.
   Please, Lord, come quickly to my aid.
      Come quickly to rescue me from these ravishing beasts.
Deliver me so that I can once again worship You
   without hindrance in the assembly of the righteous.
      Save me from my enemies
         so that I can praise You with undistracted sincerity.
      Let those who hate me without cause,
         those who ridicule me without reason,
            those who devise false accusations against me,
               those who lie about me on every occasion,
                  and those who maliciously gossip behind my back
                     be exposed for the rogues they are.

I know that You are watching all this, O God.
   You know what is going on better than I do.

Don't stand idly by.
  Come to my defense.
    Vindicate my good name.
      Contend for me.
        Don't let them gloat over me.
        Don't let them consume me.
  Give those who stand with me
    reason for hope and confidence in You.
          Give us opportunity to praise Your name for deliverance.
        Use this occasion to show Your compassion
          to those who trust in You.
          Show Your delight in the well-being
            of Your faithful servants.

Lord, I know You are listening.
  I know that You will not abandon me to my foes.
    I know that You are my help in times like this.
      I can face these trials with confidence in Your stedfast love.
  I know that I will come through this time strengthened
    in my resolve to put You first in my life.
      I know that Your deliverance will be a constant
        reminder that You are concerned with my affairs.
  I will rejoice in You continually
    and speak constantly of Your righteous care.
      I will remember You in my prayers
        with words of praise and thanksgiving.

Please, Father, bring an end to these attacks,
  And I will honor You day and night for Your deliverance.
                                        AMEN

PSALM 36

Lord, what a contrast there is between You and the wicked!

I ask for Your wisdom to recognize the deadliness of evil.
  I know that sin inevitably blinds the eyes to You, O God.
    It causes the sinner to go his way
      without regard for Your favor or Your instruction.
     He has no fear of Your judgment on him and his deeds.
     He is callous to the demands of righteousness.
  The sinner flatters himself that he is not all that bad.
    He looks at his life and takes pride
      in what little virtue he sees.
        He compares himself with others and
          says to himself that he is better than most.
    He has no ability to identify sin for what it is.
     He sees only what he chooses to see
      and he is ignorantly pleased with himself.
     He has no hatred for sin
      so his guilt does not bother him.
        He is content to be wicked.
  His mouth pours forth obscenities and lies.
   His mind is clouded;
    his actions are corrupt;
     his values are depraved.
  He neither knows nor does good.
His mind is constantly at work to promote evil.
  Day and night he is plotting some new abomination.
   He is committed to the path of sin
    and misses no opportunity to indulge his evil desires.

How unlike You, O God, is the sinner in his ways.
  You are a God of love.
    Your love overarches the heavens
     and fills the skies.
    Your love is a priceless gift
     given in spite of the unworthiness of the receiver.

Your love, so freely given, never fails.
   You are a God of righteousness.
      Your goodness is as firm as the majestic mountains
         and Your justice is as endless as the mighty seas.
   You are a God of life.
      You bring both man and beast into existence
         and You preserve them by Your daily ministration.
      You renew and sustain life
         and bring refreshment to all who seek Your living water.
   You are a God of providence.
      Without regard to social standing, reputation, or power,
         You look after the needs of those who trust in You.
      You bring peace and rest to those
         who pattern their lives after You.
         You shower them with gifts and blessings.
      You entertain them at Your table,
         giving delicious food and satisfying drink in abundance.
   You are a God of light.
      Only by Your brightness can anyone truly see.
         Only Your enlightenment can deliver from ignorance.
           Only Your illumination can dispel spiritual blindness.
      Your Word is a lamp for the path.
         Your commands are a guide through the darkness.

Please, Father, help me to be like You.
   Don't let me be blinded by the allure of wickedness.
Help me to love You with a pure and contrite heart.
   Help me to walk in faithfulness and trust.
      Bless me with Your love.
         Bless me with Your righteousness.
           Bless me with Your life.
              Bless me with Your providence.
           Bless me with Your light.
Protect me from evil people and wicked philosophies.
   Keep my feet on the upward path.
      Give me strength to withstand
         every temptation to disobedience.
         Lead me to victory
              through Your grace and power at work in me!
                   AMEN

PSALM 37

I thank You, Lord, that evil never prospers for long.
　Your Word reminds me that I need not concern myself
　　when I see wicked men and women in seeming prosperity.
　Their success will wither away.
　　Their greed will eat them up.
　　　Their wealth will turn to dust.
　　　Their power will wane.
　　　　Their businesses will fail.
　　　　　Their empires will be broken.
　　　　　　Their time for accounting will come.

O Lord, help me to trust in You.
　Help me to concentrate more on doing good
　　than on building my prestige and fame.
　Help me to deal honestly with everyone,
　　even when it means that it may cost me something.
　Help me to be the kind of person
　　I would like to do business with—
　　　understanding,
　　　　honest,
　　　　　faithful,
　　　　　　incorruptible,
　　　　　　　trustworthy,
　　　　　　　generous,
　　　　　　　　truthful,
　　　　　　　　　sincere,
　　　　　　　　　　conscientious,
　　　　　　　　　　scrupulous,
　　　　　　　　　　　honorable,
　　　　　　　　　　　unselfish.
I know that if I conduct my life with integrity,
　I will enjoy peace and what I do will prosper.
　　I will not be plagued with worry and dismay.
　　　I will enjoy the fruit of my labor.
　　　　The things I turn my mind and hands to,
　　　　　You will use to provide for my needs.

I know that if I delight in You
    You will give me the desires of my heart.

What a wonderful promise that is, Lord!
    If I put my trust in You,
        You will prosper my life beyond my fondest dreams.
        You will stand with me in my endeavors
            and see to it that my life has meaning.

O Lord, I want more than anything else to live that way.
    I don't want to live in selfishness and fear.
        I want to be filled with Your joy,
            with Your wisdom,
                with Your Spirit,
                    with Your love,
                        with Your righteousness.

O Father, I commit my life to You.
    Help me to trust You as I ought.
        I so frequently take things into my own hands.
        I so often think it is up to me to gain revenge.
            I fill my thoughts with hate for those who abuse me.
            I plot my retaliation.
                I want to get even.
   Yet, what I ought to do
        is simply to turn everything over to You.

I can trust You to put things right.
    You have promised to stand with me,
        to give my life a radiance like the sunrise.
            You will take up my cause.
            You will see that justice prevails.
    You will shed light on the secret plots of the wicked.
    You will illuminate and arbitrate in truth.

Though I know all this, Lord,
    sometimes it is very hard for me to be patient.

I get discouraged when I see evil people doing well.
  It seems as if You are not in control
    when their wicked enterprises are in the ascendency.
  I wonder if You will intervene.
    I worry lest they get away without accountability.
      I get downhearted
        and am disappointed by Your seeming uninvolvement.
  I get all agitated and upset by all that I see.

Yet, I know that this is wrong.
  It leads to no good thing.
  It merely poisons me.
I need simply to put my hope firmly in You, Lord.
  You can take care of these things much better than I can.
    I don't need to look at others with hate or envy.
      You will watch out for my interests.

The wicked are in Your hands.
  You will see to it that they get what they deserve.
    I know it is not the haughty and diabolical
      who will inherit the goodness of this life.
  Rather, it is the meek
    and lowly
      who receive all that life has to offer.
        Those who live humbly
          will live in peace,
            honor,
              love,
                and joy.

The wicked spend their days and nights hatching new schemes.
  But You laugh at all their clever plans and wicked plots.
    They think they can escape justice,
      that they are smarter than You,
        that they will succeed in their sin.
  But You, O Lord,
    are preparing their downfall.

There are always those who will take advantage
  of the poor and defenseless.
    They violate the law,
      exploit,
        gouge,
          abuse,
            cheat,
              and lie.
  They rely on force
    to terrorize the powerless.
But You, O Lord,
  will catch them in their own web of violence.
    You will break their power
      and come to the aid of the righteous.

It is better to live simply in goodness
  than to have great wealth that is gained wrongfully.
For You will make the life of the righteous invulnerable.
  Their possessions will not be taken away from them.
    Their days will be confident.
      Their ways will be without remorse.
        Their enterprises will be blessed.
  They need not fear drought or famine,
    for You watch over them with care.

The unjust are like wild flowers in the field.
  For a time they look very beautiful and impressive,
    but before long they have died and are gone.
The selfish borrow and do not return.
  They have no feelings of integrity and responsibility.
I know You want me to be different from them.
  You want me to hold my possessions lightly.
    You desire that I be generous
      with what You put in my hand.
  All that I possess is Your provision,
    so I can afford to be charitable.
  You have given me a wonderful inheritance
    to share with others who are in need.

You delight in making my path easy
and seeing to it that things go well for me.
It is true that I sometimes stumble.
Not everything is totally perfect for me.
I make mistakes
and sometimes I create problems for myself.
But You are at my side
to steady me
and put me back on my feet once again.

Father, as I grow older
I am learning more and more
to trust in You.
You will not allow the faithful
to be in want.
You will supply the needs of those who delight in You.
They needn't worry when they are generous with their resources
for You will see to it that there is enough
for both themselves and for their families.
You, O Lord, are ever with the just
to protect them and to prosper them.
You watch over their dwellings
and provide their children with an inheritance.

Help me, O Lord, to shun evil and seek good
so that You can bring stability and security to my life.
Help me to walk in justice and in faithfulness
so that You can shower Your blessings on me.

O Father, help me to watch my words
so that the utterances of my mouth
may reflect Your wisdom
and evidence Your integrity.
Help me to draw the rules of my life
from the standard of Your Word.
Help me to keep Your ordinances firmly in my mind and heart.

I know that if I rely on You
   I need not fear ruin.
      The wicked may lie in wait to harm me,
         but You will not allow them to succeed.
You will deny them their goals and dilute their power.

Help me to wait on You, Lord.
   Help me to allow You
      to handle things according to Your wisdom.
         Help me to walk in Your ways.
            Help me to be content with Your intervention.
The immoral and ruthless only flourish for a short season.
   They will pass away and be no more.
      They will be destroyed and their work will vanish.

Father, look on me with kindness.
   Help me to live a life that is upright and blameless.
      Help me to walk in peace and righteousness.
         Stand with me in my times of trouble.
            Deliver me from the snares of the deceitful.
         Save me from my sins
            and from the iniquity of others.
         Be my refuge and my strength.

For You are my loving Father,
   ever seeking to do me good.
      You are my strength in times of trouble.

Help me to be faithful.
   Help me to be genuine.
      Help me to walk in Your ways and trust You.

AMEN

PSALM 38

O Lord, don't punish me as I deserve.
  Please don't rain Your wrath upon me
    in vindication of Your justice.
      Don't crush me by the chastening
        of Your hot displeasure.
I know what it means to be out of Your favor,
  to feel as if You have become my enemy rather than my friend.
    In my innermost life there is conflict.
      I am torn with remorse.
        I am pierced with terrible fears.
          Nothing I do brings satisfaction.
            I am consumed by my failures.
      I know that I have failed You.
        I deserve Your displeasure—
          this pain of heart and mind that will not go away.

I'm sick.
  My body aches.
    My health is broken.
      It's as if there is no
        soundness at all in me, anymore.
    My bones seem to give way;
      my muscles move in torment;
        my life is plagued with despair.
          I'm crushed by the enormity of my guilt.
It's like a millstone on the neck of a drowning man.
  I cannot escape the fact that I've committed monstrous sin.

You say in Your Word that what is sown will be reaped.
  I've sown wickedness and I'm reaping wretchedness.
    Everywhere I look I see the awful results of my folly.
      My outward life is going to pieces
        and my inward life is in chaos.
There is no mistaking the cause of my anguish.
  It is sin—
    agonizing, destroying, alienating evil.

I'm like a leper.
  My open wounds fester.
    No one wants to come close to me.
      I'm a pariah—
        all because of my foolishness.
I don't know what I was thinking.
  Why did I think that sin was a matter of so little consequence?
    Why did I believe that I could get away with it
      without having to pay the cost of my folly?
I can't throw off this veil of despair.
  My body is racked with pain,
    my back is bowed down with shame.
  Day and night my transgression is on my mind.
    I cannot erase the memory of my iniquity.
      It haunts me in the darkness
        and stalks me during the light.
  My inner turmoil shows in all I do.
    I am exhausted,
      broken, crushed,
        and overwhelmed.
          I sob in shameless sorrow;
            I groan in agony of spirit.

Lord, You know me better than I know myself.
  All this is obvious to You.
    But as clearly as You know my anguish,
      You know that the desire of my heart is
        to return to Your favor.
  Oh that I could undo the sin that plagues **me!**
    Oh that my remorse could erase the past
      and heal this disease of death!
You know, O Lord, that I long with all my heart
  for forgiveness,
    for newness,
      for Your salvation.

I listen to the sounds of my turmoil.
  I hear the pounding of my heart.

My breath comes in gasps;
   the sound of death echoes in my ears.
     I gaze at my crumbling world
       through glazed eyes.
The midnight of death is settling over me.

I'm alienated from You, O God.
   I'm alienated from myself.
     I'm alienated from my friends and family.
Nobody comes to my aid
   lest the sickness of my soul
     also infect them with my dreadful disease.
I'm kept at arm's length,
   avoided,
     ignored,
       whispered about,
         held up to ridicule,
          written off.

I have no one to turn to
   in this agony of my soul.
     I'm like a deaf person,
       cut off from the sounds of consolation.
     I'm like a mute,
       unable to communicate my anguish.
     I'm bereft of all human help.
       Nothing that is said to me makes any difference.
       Nothing that I hear removes the guilt.
There is no one to help—
   no one, that is, but You.
You alone hold the key to my deliverance
   and restoration.
     I must wait on Your lovingkindness.
     I must cast myself on the altar of Your grace.

I know that You will answer my anguished prayer.
   You alone can bring relief, renewal, and forgiveness.
     You alone can restore health to my ravaged soul.

O Lord, hear the prayer of my repentance,
   bind up my brokenness,
      cleanse me of my corruption.

Father, don't let our enemies rejoice in my sin.
   Help me to turn even this lapse
      into a message of Your love and grace.
I'm hanging on, waiting for You to pull me to safety.

Father, I confess to You my sin.
   I ask your forgiveness.
      I know that what I have done is wrong.
         I ask Your help that I might not fall into
         the trap of this evil again.
I know that all the trouble I have caused
   by my sin will not go away immediately.
      Though You forgive me,
         I must still live with the memory of my transgression.
         There will be many people
            and many things
               to remind me of my folly.
No matter how I try to undo what I have done
   I will still have to live with the suspicions
      of those who will ascribe evil motives to my every action.
I have tarnished the trust
   that I once knew in my relationships with others.

O Lord, be near me.
   You are my sole resting place.
      Let me know Your presence,
         in this time of penance.
            Come quickly to my rescue.
            You are my help.
               You are my hope.
                  You are my salvation.

AMEN

PSALM 39

Dear Lord, sometimes I bottle up my praise.
   I keep silent when I'm around unbelievers
      and I watch my words lest I offend them.
   But I can't keep Your goodness to myself.
      When I try, I find my life is empty
         and my woes multiply.
   The more I think of You,
      the more my soul is warmed by Your love.

Father, help me to realize how brief life is.
   Help me to set worthy goals
      for I have so little time
         to accomplish Your purposes.
   Show me for what I've been created
      so that I may fulfill my divine destiny.

The world seems to spin faster each year I live.
   Time races by
      and I accomplish so few of my dreams.
Yet, You are eternal!
   Compared to You I am a split second in eternity.
      I'm a short breath,
         a quick gasp,
            a brief breeze,
               a glowing spark quickly quenched.
   I rush about,
      busy myself,
         struggle and strive,
            brag and swagger,
               and heap up monuments to my importance,
                  but all my activity is, in the end, futile.
   I open my bank accounts,
      and buy my houses,
         and invest in my stocks and bonds,
            but when all is said and done,
               I will leave everything behind.

I'm learning to keep my eyes on You.
  I know You alone are my hope for eternity.
    Forgive my sins and deliver me from futility.
  I am speechless before You.
    I have no insight or wisdom
      that You have not given me.
        You are the source of all meaning in my life.
  Give me a heart to do Your will.
    Encourage me with Your direction;
      control me with Your power;
        enfold me with Your love.
Your guidance is my sole source of satisfaction.
  Your discipline brings only good to my life.
    All my accomplishments count for nothing with You.
      My tale is told in triviality;
        my brief life is ordered by Your grace.

Hear my prayer, O Lord.
  I need Your help.
    I so often feel alienated,
      alone,
        disoriented,
          unnoticed,
            inconsequential,
              abandoned.
  Look upon me with love.
    Help me to rejoice with every heartbeat
      You give me until the day
        I come to dwell eternally with You.

AMEN

PSALM 40

O Lord, You have done wondrous things for me.
  When I have been in the depths of despair,
    You have come to my rescue
      and restored me to joy and confidence once again.
    You have responded to my prayers
      and brought comfort and stability to my life.
    You have replaced my moanings of misery
      with glad songs of thanksgiving and praise.

Help me to be patient as I meet my trials.
  In my difficulties, help me to point others toward You.
    In my troubles, help me to rely totally on You.
      I know I will be blessed beyond belief
        if I trust You implicitly for the future.

Yet, I am so prone to put my trust in false gods—
  friends, family,
    education, reputation,
      ability, accomplishment,
        job, knowledge.
I am sometimes too proud to admit that I need You
  and what You offer me.
    My attention seems to center on the difficulties I face
      and my human resources to overcome them,
        rather than on Your love and care for me.

I am awed by the wonderful things You have done for me
  and have planned for me in the future.
    They surpass my comprehension.

You are not particularly impressed
  with my ostentatious efforts to conform
    to the outward appearance of holiness.
  Rather, You desire that I hear and do Your Word.
    You seek for me to be responsive to Your leading.
      You want Your law to be written in my heart.

O that I could proclaim Your righteousness
  with imagination and creative discourse
    so that all who hear might know You, O Lord.
Let me speak boldly of Your faithfulness and salvation,
  Your goodness and holiness.
    I depend upon Your mercy, O Lord.
Your love and truth protect me
  from the innumerable troubles that surround me.

I am often blinded by my transgressions.
  I become weak and frightened when I think of my sins.
    I am ashamed of my foolish willfulness,
      embarrassed by the enormity of my wickedness.
There is no one but You to help in matters of the spirit.
  I know that You have compassion for me
    and that You will come quickly to deliver me.
      You stand by my side
        and confuse and thwart those who seek to do me harm.

Lord, I know that seeking You
  is the path of joy and gladness.
    You are the source of my salvation,
      my keeper from harm,
        my friend in times of need.
You are exalted above all else that is,
  yet You stoop to love me.

I am nobody without You—
  poor, needy, oppressed, powerless.
    Yet, You are mindful of me.
      You come to my aid and deliver me;
        You surround me with Your wonders.
O God, I would like to be patient
  in waiting for the answer to my prayers.
    But it is hard to wait sometimes, Father.
      Please work Your wonders as quickly as possible.
                                              AMEN

PSALM 41

Lord, I thank You that You have
   a special fondness for the weak.
     I thank You that You come to their aid with deliverance,
       that You protect them,
         and that You keep them from disaster.
     You preserve their lives,
       bless them with contentment,
         and protect them from their foes.

Father, the foe of my life right now is sickness.
   My body is racked with pain
     and my mind is anxious for the future.
   All I can think of is my illness,
     its meaning,
       its consequences,
         its frustrations,
           its fears.
Lord, I know I am a sinner
   and that I need spiritual as well
     as physical healing.
       Cleanse me from the wickedness of my heart.
       Purge me from the cancer of the sins
         that multiply to choke out my life.
Heal me, O Father,
   from maladies of body *and* spirit.

My enemies delight in my misery, and rejoice in my pain.
   And though my friends come to see me,
     they are more interested
       in spreading the news of my problems
       than in ministering to my hurt.
Secretly, they are glad that I am brought low,
   for they interpret my suffering as their vindication.
     They are sayers of doom.
       They bring no hope or encouragement.
       They can't wait for me to die.

Even my closest friends—
    the people in whom I have confided through the years,
        those who have shared food at my table—
            they seem to have departed from me as well.

But You, O Lord, are stedfast!
    Though all others forsake me, You never leave me.
I can trust You with my failures,
    I can lean on You in my infirmities,
        I can find encouragement in Your lovingkindness.

When I am in Your will,
    no enemy can vanquish me.
        When I walk in honesty and truth,
            You are by my side.
                When my heart is open before You,
                    Your presence preserves me.

I praise You, O eternal, loving Father,
    for not forsaking me in my trial.
        You will deliver me from my affliction
            and restore me once again to gladness.

O Lord, I thank You that You have a
    special love for me in my weakness!

AMEN

PSALM 42

My soul pants for You, O Lord,
  like a deer pants for a sparkling brook
    to quench its thirst in the midday heat.
      I want to know Your presence;
        I yearn to experience renewal in You;
          I long to commune deeply with You;
            I desire to walk in Your will.
You are the source, center, and goal of my life,
  the proper object of my praise,
    my closest friend in time of need.

You know that right now I am seeking You in tears.
  It seems as if I can't stop their flow,
    no matter what I do.
I can't seem to find any consolation or sympathy from others.
  They use the occasion of my grief
    to undercut my faith in You.
  "Where is Your God," they say, "when You need Him most?"
My tears flow like a mountain spring—day and night.

I try to focus my mind on the good days of the past.
  I remember how joyous I was when I joined in praise
    and sang the songs of faith and trust
      with a host of believers within Your sanctuary.
  I looked forward to worship then—
    the expressions of joy and thanksgiving,
      the consciousness of Your presence,
        the lifting of my spirit in adoration,
        the exuberance of prayer.

I don't know why I've let things get to me as they have.
  My hope is in You, O God.
    I know that I'll come through this depression
      and will return to the delight of Your praise once again.
    I know this sorrow is a temporary disturbance,
      not a permanent disaster.

I've learned in the past that when I'm in the pits,
  I need to lift my eyes to You, O Father.
I need to raise my eyes from the dark valley of my troubles
  to the high mountain
    of Your love for me.
As mighty rivers burst forth from the base
  of soaring peaks,
    Your refreshment pours out
      to bless and sustain me.
  You send Your cool consolation
    to sweep over me and relieve my aching spirit.

Communion with You is so sweet, Lord.
  Day and night I find my rest in You.
    Your love overshadows me in the heat of the day,
      Your majesty fills me with confident song
        in the long night watches.
  You are my God,
    the firm foundation of my life.
      You do not forget me when I am discouraged.
  You share in my despair,
    even when it seems as if my agony will never end.

I will pay no heed to those
  who deny You and ridicule my faith in You.
    I know that You are here
      even when I feel most forsaken.
I know that the way to overcome this depression
  is to praise You, my Savior and my God.
You are my sure source of hope,
  and I will trust in You whatever happens.
    You will never forget me,
      or forsake me,
        or allow me to fall.
You quench my thirst for meaning and purpose.
  You refresh me with living water!

AMEN

PSALM 43

Lord, I'm disturbed!
  I'm surrounded by ugliness,
    deceitfulness,
      and wickedness.
  I live in a world that seems to run on lies,
    extortion,
      fraud,
        exploitation,
          inhumanity,
            oppression,
              deceit,
                and duplicity.

I get so discouraged
  as I read the morning news
    and listen to the evening reports.
Nations subvert one another,
  arming themselves to crush the innocent,
    sowing seeds of rebellion,
      torturing the weak and helpless.
My world is violent and unprincipled.
  My nation is morally corrupt.
    My city is a place of violence.
    My home is no longer safe.
      My heart is contaminated with evil desires.

Father, help me to stay pure
  in the midst of all this evil.
    Help me to stand for truth and righteousness
      in the face of this ever-present depravity.

I can't do it without You, Father.
  You alone are my strength and my sanctuary.
    You alone give me wisdom and understanding.
      You alone protect me from the evil
        that threatens to suffocate me.

If You are not with me,
 my life is filled with pain,
  timidity,
   defeat,
    sadness,
     and remorse.
But when I am in tune with You,
 my life is lived in harmony and joy.
  When I am illuminated by Your light
  and counseled by Your truth,
   I walk through life with confidence.
You welcome me into Your presence.
 You enfold me in Your love.
  You lift me up from despair.
  You fill my days with delight.

O God, Your light dispels the darkness of this sinful world.
 Your truth supplies a fixed standard for all moral judgment.
When I walk in Your light and am guided by Your will,
 I have no reason to fear
  what may befall me in this derelict world.
  I can lift my heart and voice in songs
   of praise for Your guidance and deliverance.
   I can delight in You
    and experience Your presence.

O God, *You* are my hope!
 I've set my heart to praise You
  in the midst of this corrupt world.
   You lift me out of degradation
    and plant my feet
     on the mountain of holiness.
  You bring me repose in the midst of encircling woe.
   You give my life purpose and meaning.
   You are my Savior and my God.
The future is in Your hands.
 I will trust You with my little portion of it!

AMEN

PSALM 44

O God, history is full of Your mighty acts.
  We read of them on every page of Your revealed Word.
    You chose a people and molded them into a great nation.
    You stood by them in times of adversity.
      You conquered their foes
        and gave them a wonderful land to call their own.
    You hand seemed to be upon them;
      Your blessing was with them.

I know it was not by their strength or wisdom
  that they prevailed in the midst of difficult circumstances.
    It wasn't their swords that slew the enemies.
      It wasn't their armor that protected them from death.
        It wasn't their strength that kept them standing upright.
          It wasn't their arrows that brought to nothing
            the might of their adversaries.
    It was You with them that made the difference, O God.
      It was You with them that brought success
        against all odds.
  You pushed the enemy back before them.
    You decreed victory and it came to pass.
      You were a strong King to rule and protect them.
      You were a mighty God to love and cherish them.

Help me to learn, dear Lord, not to put my trust
  in instruments of my devising.
    My inclination is to think that I can provide for the future,
      that all that really matters is what I do,
        and how I plan and prepare,
          and what I provide for every eventuality.

But I know all that is nothing if You are not with me.
  You are the one who grants success.
    You are the one who protects me from disaster.
      You are the one who comes to my aid
        and brings to pass all that is good in my life.

I need to acknowledge You in all that I do.
   I need to praise You and thank You for all good things.
     I have so little to do with how things end.
Help me to acknowledge Your providence each day of my life.
   Help me to praise Your name with every breath You give me.

I know all this, O God.
   History is full of Your glory.
     The divine record is true and clear.
But I can't understand *what is happening to me just now.*
   I'm not experiencing the kind of victory
     Your dealings with Israel lead me to expect.
   It seems as if I am living in defeat rather than triumph.
     Instead of being a conqueror,
       I am being conquered by every difficulty.
   The enemy seems to be winning.
     Instead of standing upright with confidence,
       I am being thrown down and trampled by every adversary.
   It seems as if You are on the side of my foes.
     I am in retreat before my troubles.
       I cannot point to my life
         as an example of Your strength and Your help.
   I feel as if I've been sold out to the enemy,
     that I'm at the mercy of predators,
       that I'm coming apart at the seams,
         that I just can't keep it all together.

I feel so lost and abandoned!
   Everybody seems to be laughing at me.
     I can't hold my head up.
       Rather, I mope and worry about what others
         think and say about me.
     I can't get my mind off myself and my troubles.
       My song of celebration is a dirge;
         my bugle is sounding retreat;
           my flag is lying in the dust.
Quite honestly, Lord,
   I can't figure out why this is happening to me.

I've searched my heart and life
  and I have found no hidden sin there.
    I'm not going after other gods.
      I'm not living in sin
        or disregarding Your commandments.
  My desire is still to do Your will,
    as it has always been.
  I can't see why it is necessary for You to punish me.
    I can't see why Your discipline is called for
      in my present circumstances.
    It just doesn't add up to me, O Father.
      Yet, this darkness of despair and defeat
        has swept over me and I know
          that there must be a reason for it all.
If I were living in disobedience,
  I could understand the reasons for Your disfavor.
    If I were living a lie in my adoration of You,
      I could understand and expect Your wrath.
  Yet, I feel, somehow, that I am suffering innocently.

Could it be, Father,
  that You are teaching me some of the experience of Jesus?
    Could You be allowing me to know
      what it was like for Jesus to hang on the cross,
        not for His sins, but for mine?
  Do You want me to learn that there is not a direct
    cause and effect relationship between prosperity, success,
      and relationship with You?
  Are You trying to teach me that the faithful
    sometimes suffer too?
  Are You reminding me that the most perfect and loving
    human being that ever existed
      nevertheless bore suffering and shame
        because of His love for You and for me?

Are You helping me to know that good people often suffer?
  That virtue does not always triumph in this life?
    And that the righteous are not always materially blessed?

Lord,
  I know that my present condition will not always prevail.
    You will use even these problems
      to glorify Your name.
        You will bring victory and hope
          into my life once more.
  You will turn again to me with deliverance.
  You will yet shower me with blessing.
    You have not forgotten my misery and oppression.
    You are not unmindful
      of my exhaustion,
        my failure,
          my collapse,
            my mistakes.

You will not leave me in the depths for long.
  I know, O Lord, that Your love
    will lift me up from the dust of my defeat
    and set me on the rock of rejoicing.

Come to my rescue, Lord.
  Come soon.

AMEN

PSALM 45

O Lord God, You inspire me
  to thoughts and expressions of praise.

You stir my spirit to contemplate
  the wonder of Jesus, my Lord and King.
  You fill my poetry and prose
    with words of awe and appreciation
      for all that You have done for me in Christ.
  I just cannot comprehend
    the magnificence of Your grace,
      the blessings of Your love.

Jesus came—
  a man apart,
    above,
      beyond all humanity,
  yet a man, nevertheless—
    Your very essence clothed in human flesh.
His words were seasoned with grace.
  He spoke of life,
    and hope,
      and faith,
        and love as no one had ever spoken before.
          You blessed Him—
            and the world through Him.

He was clothed in majesty and splendor.
  He possessed all Your might,
    yet He walked gently in this world of sinners.
      He was totally Yours,
        completely given over to doing Your will.
      He spoke in truth and righteousness,
        though many laid snares for Him.
He healed the sick
  and raised the dead,
    and took the part of the outcast and oppressed.

Though He died on the cross,
yet He rose in victory.
He put death to flight,
conquering by His own suffering
the last enemy of all mankind.

He alone is worthy of absolute praise.
He alone is Lord of all.
He alone is the Redeemer of the world.
His rule is forever;
His justice is true;
His righteousness is untarnished.
He is Your anointed one,
a King of justice and joy.
He rules in majesty.
He reigns in grandeur.
His greatness inspires me with awe and gladness.
With thanksgiving I join the great company of worshipers
who fall before Him in homage and adoration.

O let the church, His bride, be faithful to Him.
Let her forsake all others and cleave to Him totally.
Let the church honor Him with every thought and action.
Let the church be beautiful,
like a bride on her wedding day.
Let her be pure and holy,
drawing her joy and gladness
from her relationship with her Husband, her King.
Let the church be fruitful.
Let her dedicate herself to honoring Jesus Christ
and proclaiming His greatness throughout the land.
Let the church be a fountain of praise,
a wellspring of adoration.
Let her impact on human history
so that all peoples
in all places
will come to know the Lord!

AMEN

PSALM 46

O God, You are my refuge and strength.
You are my helper in times of trouble.
You are my confidence and courage.
Because of You, I am free from fear.
My world can tremble beneath my feet,
my mountain refuge can fall into the sea,
my quiet seashore can be dashed by the hurricane
—but I will not be afraid.

You make me joyful, O God!
I will take up residence in Your domain.
You are my fortress.
You are my constant help.
I look to You for deliverance and victory.
Thank you for welcoming me into Your city,
for honoring me with Your presence,
for supplying my need for refreshment,
for gladdening my heart with Your rule.

The whole world seems on the verge of collapse.
Terrorism threatens on every hand.
Nations rise and fall.
Natural calamities ravage the earth.

Yet, I know that You are with the faithful.
You do not abandon Your chosen ones in times of distress.
You are Lord of life,
Almighty indweller,
and protector of believers.

I marvel when I think of all Your mighty works.
You change the face of the earth when it pleases You.
You subdue nations and initiate peace.
When it pleases You,
You destroy the mighty war machines
in which nations blindly put their confidence.

Father God, help me to listen quietly to Your voice.
　Help me to learn more of You in the solitude
　　as well as in the ceaseless activity of life.
　I know that You are supreme ruler of all,
　　absolute monarch of the whole world.

Thank You for Your promises to the faithful.
　Thank You for being my strong defense.
　Thank You for caring about what happens to me.

Lord, You are with me constantly.
　I thank You for the sense of gladness
　　and security this gives me.
　I thank You for the excellence
　　with which You constantly envelop me.

AMEN

PSALM 47

I come before You with joy and gladness, O Lord God.
  I want to shout in exaltation of Your glorious name.
    I want to lift my voice in songs of praise.
You are King over all the earth.
  There is no one in all the universe to compare with You.
    I stand in awe before Your greatness.
You have given me victory in the conflicts of my life.
    You have made me heir to Your glorious inheritance.
      You have loved me with an everlasting love.

Your praise is my sole vocation in life.
  You alone are worthy of honor.
    You came into my heart in triumphant procession
      to rule as Lord and King.
My heart sings Your praise.
  My voice lifts up Your name with adoration.
    My heart speaks forth Your lovingkindness.
All creation speaks Your greatness.
  The birds chirp a carol of Your grandeur;
    the islands of the sea shout a chanty of Your infinitude;
      the mountains intone a melody of Your majesty;
        the nations of the world proclaim Your just rule.

You are the object of all worship.
  You are the center of all creation.
    You are the sovereign of all nations.
      You are the source of all life.
        You are the creator of all that is.
I will exalt You.
  I will sing Your praise.
    I will seek Your counsel.
      I will lift my voice to You in admiration.
        I will speak aloud of Your wondrous nature.
        I will rest secure in Your wise rule.
You are Lord Most High,
  the great King over all the earth!

AMEN

PSALM 48

O Lord, I love to meditate upon Your greatness.
   You are wonderful beyond my imaginings.
      Your glory fills the whole of creation.
      You are worthy of my praise,
         the rightful object of my thanksgiving.

I love to dwell in Your city,
   to survey Your mighty citadels,
      to gaze at Your beautiful works,
         to take my joy in Your presence.
Thank You for reaching down to man,
   for communicating Your truth to Your chosen,
      for protecting the faithful and for overcoming my foes.
I am always secure because I dwell with You.
   Your love is my strong defense.
      Your righteousness is my hope.
      Your judgments are my joy.

I love to meditate on Your greatness,
   to contemplate Your mighty acts.
      I enjoy telling of Your wonderful deeds
      to my children,
         to my friends,
            to my acquaintances,
            to my neighbors.
You are a God of worthiness,
   excellence,
      loftiness,
         celebration,
            power,
               protection,
                  confidence,
                     love,
                        righteousness,
                          mercy and guidance
                          both now and forever.

You are *my* God.
  You take a personal interest in my affairs,
    in my conduct,
      in my righteousness,
        in my goals,
          in my priorities,
            in my faithfulness,
              in my happiness,
                in my fulfillment,
                  and in my relationships.

Please guide me in the way of life, O my God!
  And may I follow Your leading
    with loyalty, patience, and courage.

AMEN

PSALM 49

O Lord, give me wisdom.
Help me to understand the ways of life.
Give me clearsightedness in a world of illusion.

It seems as if so much of the world is governed by greed.
People long for wealth
and the power it gives them over others.
Our world seems to reward greed
and to lionize those who achieve financial success,
no matter how they achieve it.
But money doesn't buy Your approval.
You are not impressed by our bank accounts.
You cannot be bribed with our wealth.
Your redemption is not for sale to the highest bidder.
The wealthy will die just as certainly as the poor.
The aristocrat goes into the grave
just as penniless as the pauper.

Sometimes I think, O Lord,
that I'm going to be an exception.
It's true that all people die,
but I keep telling myself
it won't happen to me.
I hold on to things as if they are truly mine,
yet I know that one day they will be auctioned to strangers
on the very property I have called my own.
I try to deny death,
and create elaborate euphemisms
to keep from staring it in the face.
Yet, it is on the agenda
just as surely for me
as it is for the dumb animal
that grazes in the field.
All my wisdom and accomplishments
won't make any difference in my ability
to hang onto life indefinitely.

How foolish I am to think that I can somehow cheat death!
  Death already has me in its grasp.
    I see it in my greying hair,
      my sagging skin,
        my slowing reflexes.

Yet, I know that death does not have the last word
  for the upright of heart.
    Death is the gateway to Your presence
      and the pathway to Your eternal kingdom.

I don't need to envy the rich and famous.
  When they stand before You,
    their earthly prosperity and influence
      will obtain no special favors from You.
  Their pride and their prestige
    will provide no protection from death.
      The grave will claim them just as surely
        as it did their ancestors.
  For all their great fame and fortune,
    their lives are just as fragile
      as that of the most insignificant animals.

O Lord, give me wisdom.
  Help me to understand the ways of life.
    Give me clearsightedness in a world of illusion.

AMEN

PSALM 50

O God Almighty, I want to know You!
    Help me not to become sidetracked in my religious life.
        It is so easy for me to substitute outward form
            for inner faithfulness.
                Give me purity of heart and life, O God.

I know that You judge the earth,
    assessing and evaluating all human action.
Your judgment is like a mighty forest fire devouring all before it.
    It is like a tornado destroying everything in its path.
        None can escape Your scrutiny.
            We all must give account of our faithfulness.

I know, mighty Father, that You have no need for my sacrifices.
    You are my God and all things belong to You.
        You don't need my puny gifts.
            What can I bring You that You did not make,
                that You do not already possess,
                    that You do not put in my hand?
        You have no need for me to take care of You.
        But I need You to take care of me.
Help me to come before You with thanksgiving.
    Help me to be true to my vows.
        Help me to pray diligently for deliverance.
            Help me to honor You consistently in word and deed.

If I don't obey Your Word,
    it does me no good to recite Your commands
        and preach rousing homilies on the fine points of doctrine.
If I am disobedient in heart,
    You are not pleased with my instruction of others,
        no matter how eloquent or forceful my words may be.
If I am hypocritical,
    giving lip service to Your instruction
        while secretly joining the wicked in their evil deeds,
            You will eventually expose my folly.